Fight Like the Devil

THE FIRST DAY AT GETTYSBURG
JULY 1, 1863

By Chris Mackowski
Kristopher D. White
and Daniel T. Davis

EMERGING CIVIL WAR SERIES

Chris Mackowski, series editor
Kristopher D. White, chief historian

Also part of the Emerging Civil War Series:

Fight Like the Devil

THE FIRST DAY AT GETTYSBURG
JULY 1, 1863

By Chris Mackowski
Kristopher D. White
and Daniel T. Davis

EMERGING CIVIL WAR SERIES

SB
Savas Beatie
California

Second edition, first printing

ISBN-13: 978-1-61121-227-3

Library of Congress Cataloging-in-Publication Data

Mackowski, Chris.
    Fight like the devil : the first day at Gettysburg, July 1, 1863 / by Chris Mackowski, Kristopher D. White, and Daniel T. Davis. -- First edition.
    pages cm. -- (Emerging civil war series)
    ISBN 978-1-61121-227-3 (pbk. : alk. paper)
    1. Gettysburg, Battle of, Gettysburg, Pa., 1863. I. White, Kristopher D. II. Davis, Daniel T., 1982- III. Title.
    E475.53.M127 2015
    973.7'349--dc23
    2014045711

Published by
Savas Beatie LLC
989 Governor Drive, Suite 102
El Dorado Hills, California 95762
Phone: 916-941-6896
Email: sales@savasbeatie.com
Web: www.savasbeatie.com

Savas Beatie titles are available at special discounts for bulk purchases in the United States by corporations, institutions, and other organizations. For more details, please contact Special Sales, P.O. Box 4527, El Dorado Hills, CA 95762, or you may e-mail us as at sales@savasbeatie.com, or visit our website at www.savasbeatie.com for additional information.

CHRIS: *To my siblings: my brother, Matt, and my cousins Amish and Sarah T, who all grew up with me around this battlefield.*

KRIS: *To Unc and Aunt Nancy, without whom I may never have stepped foot on the Gettysburg Battlefield.*

DAN: *For Uncle Bill*

We jointly dedicate this book to our lovely wives

Table of Contents

List of Maps

Maps by Hal Jespersen

Acknowledgments

We work with some great Civil War historians at Emerging Civil War. Among them, Eric Wittenberg, Chris Kolakowski, David Powell, Meg Thompson, Phill Greenwalt, and Ryan Quint were specifically helpful with this volume. Dan Welch with the Gettysburg Foundation stepped up to offer invaluable

assistance in many ways as we finished this manuscript. Thanks, too, to Matt Atkinson and James Brookes for their appendices and to Hal Jespersen, whose maps continue to enhance the entire book series.

At Savas Beatie, Theodore P. Savas keeps the torches lit for us. He has a wonderful and supportive staff. Thanks, in particular, to Yvette and Michele and our proofreader, Mary Holuta. Sarah Keeney continues to serves as the Emerging Civil War Series's "eternal light."

The 17th Pennsylvania Cavalry monument (above); the 6th New York Cavalry monument (opposite) (cm)

Finally, we were extremely fortunate to benefit from the insights and assistance of the gracious Mark Dunkelman, whose widely respected work on the 154th New York has taught us all so much about the war in general from the regimental level. Thank you!

CHRIS: Kris White is the spiritual godfather of this volume and the Gettysburg volumes that will follow. As someone who grew up on the Gettysburg battlefield and as a former Licensed Battlefield Guide, Kris has a deep and profound love for this hallowed ground, which he has always wanted to share.

I have worked with Dan Davis for years, but never as a writing partner. Now I am asking myself, "What took so long?" What an energizing experience!

At St. Bonaventure University's Russell J. Jandoli School of Journalism and Mass Communication, I thank my dean, Dr. Pauline Hoffmann. I thank my students, too—who sometimes wonder about all this Civil War stuff I do. But it's all this writing that gives me the credibility to go into their classrooms and teach them how to write.

My first visit to Gettysburg came as a field trip with Mr. Leader's third-grade class from Hershey Elementary School. I have a picture of a bunch of us hanging on one of the cannons on Oak Hill. I experienced the field that day with such great folks as Bob and Katie McKinney Gavazzi, Ellen Kellner, Bobby Mittan, Audrey Buglione, Andy Shrawder, Christine Zoumas, Sheila Duggan Kettlewell, Scott Cranston, and so many more. A special shout-out to two of my oldest friends from those days, Anthony Elby and Kelly Ramsden-Herr.

On July 1, 2013, as part of sesquicentennial coverage of the battle of Gettysburg, I returned to Oak Hill as one of several talking heads interviewed for cable TV coverage of events. My wife, Jennifer, came with me—except she wasn't my wife yet. In fact, this was one of our first dates. She sat in a canvas chair off to the side and did some work she brought with her and listened as I did my schtick. Afterwards, we went for some Tommy's Pizza. All in all, not a bad day considering the way things turned out. I'm sure it was the Tommy's that saved me.

Finally, to my children, Stephanie and Jackson, who remain my High Water marks.

KRIS: My deepest thanks goes to both Chris and Dan. These two great friends are the reason this work saw the light of day. I am deeply indebted to them both for taking up the torch and seeing the project to fruition. Words cannot adequately express my gratitude.

DAN: It is an honor and privilege to finally work with Kris and Chris. I owe them both a debt of gratitude for everything they have done for me. All I can say is "thank you."

I cannot thank my lovely wife Katy enough for her love and ongoing support. She continues to be a source of inspiration. To my mom and dad, Kathy and Tommy Davis, who took my brother, Matt, and me to Gettysburg when we were very young. Over the years, I have visited the battlefield with my aunt and uncle, Margie and Butch Markham, just as much as with my parents.

I also need to extend a thanks to my pard and co-author, Phillip Greenwalt, who is always available as a sounding board and to discuss the Civil War. Finally, for my Great Uncle Bill, whose trips and remembrances of Gettysburg continue to be a topic of our weekly conversations.

(cm)

PHOTO CREDITS: Adams County Historical Society (achs); John Cummings (jc); Dan Davis (dd); Mark H. Dunkelman (md); Gettysburg Daily (gd); Gettysburg National Military Park (gnmp); Philip Greenwalt (pg); Library of Congress (loc); Chris Mackowski (cm); John Maginn (jm); National Park Service (nps); Michael Waricher (mw); Dan Welch (dw).

(*) The photo of Howard on the Fahnestock building on pg. 69 from *A Boy's Experience During the Battles of Gettysburg* by Daniel Alexander Skelly (Gettysburg: Daniel Alexander Skelly, 1932), courtesy of Gettysburg National Military Park.

(**) The photo of FDR on pg. 154 owned by Ralph Gardner, Harrisburg, Pa., and loaned by Wm. M. Schmick, Enola, Pa., courtesy of Gettysburg National Military Park.

For the Emerging Civil War Series

Theodore P. Savas, *publisher*
Chris Mackowski, *series editor and co-founder*
Kristopher D. White, *chief historian and co-founder*
Sarah Keeney, *editorial consultant*   Maps by Hal Jespersen
Daniel T. Davis, *emeritus editor*   Design and layout by Chris Mackowski

Touring the Battlefield

The same road network that converged on Gettysburg as the Adams County seat—which, in turn, brought the armies here—still services a great many people. For battlefield visitors, those roads can both help and hinder a tour of the battlefield, especially in the town itself, which often bustles with tourists, college students, and of course, the gracious residents who put up with "invasions" of people year after year. Please be considerate and be careful.

The organization of this book and tour reflects knowledge of the local roads and also takes into consideration related information such as National Park Service facilities, the availability of parking, and local spots of congestion. The roads remain busy, and in the town, the streets can sometimes be narrow and have limited visibility, especially at intersections.

Please also note that some park roads are one way. All park roads and trails receive year-round maintenance. They close each night at dusk.

In keeping with the actions of July 1, the tour in this book focuses on the north end of the battlefield. However, we encourage visitors to explore the full park as they're able. Gettysburg is a wonderful town with many sites to see and places to explore. We particularly encourage visitors to walk around downtown, as well as explore the shops along Steinwehr Avenue.

Gen. Wadsworth points the way (dd)

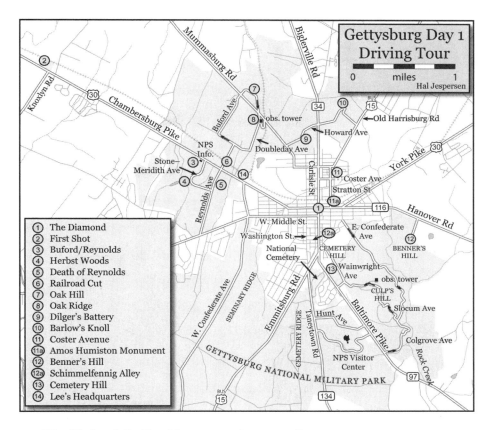

Gettysburg Day 1
Driving Tour

0   miles   1
Hal Jespersen

1. The Diamond
2. First Shot
3. Buford/Reynolds
4. Herbst Woods
5. Death of Reynolds
6. Railroad Cut
7. Oak Hill
8. Oak Ridge
9. Dilger's Battery
10. Barlow's Knoll
11. Coster Avenue
11a. Amos Humiston Monument
12. Benner's Hill
12a. Schimmelfennig Alley
13. Cemetery Hill
14. Lee's Headquarters

The National Park's visitor center is an excellent place to get additional resources and employ a Licensed Battlefield Guide. For a focus on the first day and the civilian experience, we encourage a stop at the Seminary Ridge Museum.

This photograph of the main building of the Lutheran Theological Seminary was taken some two short weeks after the end of the battle by photographer Matthew Brady. At the time of the photo, the building was still in use as a hospital. (loc)

Foreword

BY MARK H. DUNKELMAN

Like a well-crafted drama, the battle of Gettysburg unfolded in three distinct phases: beginning, middle, and end. Until recent decades, historians generally downplayed the fighting of July 1, 1863, dismissing it as a mere prelude to the combats of July 2 and 3.

Several factors combined to aim the spotlight on Days Two and Three while casting Day One into shadow. One was the very nature of the First Day's fight, which began as a meeting engagement before escalating into a full-scale encounter. Another was the proportion of the contending armies that was involved: about one-quarter of the Union Army of the Potomac and one-third of the Confederate Army of Northern Virginia were engaged on July 1, whereas both armies were present in full on the next two days. Furthermore, the First Day's combat was geographically remote from the rest of the battlefield. McPherson Woods, Oak Ridge, Blocher's Knoll, and Kuhn's Brickyard did not become instantly recognizable landmarks like Cemetery Hill, Devil's Den, Little Round Top, and the Copse of Trees. Relatively few photographs, for example, were taken soon after the battle on the fields of the First Day. Finally, July 1 marked a major tactical victory for the Confederates—an anomaly in the overall battle, which resulted in their unequivocal defeat.

Recently, however, historians have come to appreciate and emphasize the importance of the First Day at Gettysburg. By holding back the Confederates for more than eight hours, the Union forces prevented them from occupying the heights south of the town, setting the stage for the events that followed. True, fewer combatants were engaged on July 1 than on July 2 and 3—two Union corps faced four Confederate divisions (who came to outnumber the Federals almost two to one)—but they fought for a longer period than on the next two days, from early in the morning (with a midday lull) until late afternoon. And the casualties among those engaged were

Mark Dunkelman's mural depicting the Kuhn brickyard fight (md)

staggering: roughly 60 percent for the Federals and 37 percent for the Confederates. The two Union corps that fought on the First Day—the I and XI—were irretrievably damaged by their losses.

The First Day's conflict is rich in controversies. From 1863 to today, students of the battle have grappled with numerous intriguing questions. Was a fight at Gettysburg inevitable? Did a search for shoes bring the Confederates to the town? Did a poor performance by the XI Corps doom the Union effort? Did Confederate general John B. Gordon meet Union general Francis C. Barlow on the battlefield, or is the tale a legend? And asked most frequently: Could the Confederates have taken Cemetery Hill that evening, after driving the Yankees to its shelter?

The First Day also yielded two of the battle's best-known human interest stories: the tale of John Burns, the septuagenarian veteran of the War of 1812 who took up his musket and joined the Union line to defend his hometown, and that of Sgt. Amos Humiston, who died clutching a photograph of his three children—the clue that led to the identification of him and his family and inspired a flood of heartfelt poetry, song, and accounts from sympathizers throughout the North.

Sergeant Humiston's regiment, the 154th New York Volunteer Infantry, offers a fine example of how historians' coverage of the First Day has expanded in recent years. The 154th fought at Kuhn's Brickyard on the afternoon of July 1 in an action that pitted one Union brigade against two brigades of Confederates. The short but brutal conflict resulted in more than 770 casualties on both sides. Edwin B. Coddington, in his classic 1968 study of the campaign and battle of Gettysburg, summarized the brickyard fight in a couple of sentences. More than three decades later, in his 2001 book on the First Day, historian Harry W. Pfanz devoted an entire chapter to the brickyard battle.

Chris Mackowski, Kris White, and Dan Davis have studied and absorbed the fine recent histories of the First Day. In the following pages, they offer a concise account and a cogent analysis that serves as a splendid introduction to the momentous events that unfolded north and west of Gettysburg on July 1, 1863.

Mark H. Dunkelman, *the regimental historian for the 154th New York Infantry, painted a mural depicting the regiment's fight in Kuhn's brickyard on July 1, 1863 (above). The mural can be seen along Coster Avenue in Gettysburg. Dunkelman is also the author of several books, and he maintains a website about the 154th, www.hardtackregiment.com.*

AN ENDURING LIGHT
TO GUIDE US IN
UNITY AND FELLOWSHIP

"You will have to fight like the devil to hold your own. . . ."

— *Maj. Gen. John Buford*

(cm)

The First Battle of Gettysburg

PROLOGUE
JUNE 26, 1863

The sound of thundering hooves reverberated through the streets as two hundred and sixty two men of Lt. Col. Elijah V. White's 35th Virginia Battalion of Cavalry—known as White's Comanches—came bounding in from the west along Chambersburg Street. After making their way into Gettysburg's town square, the Diamond, they scattered in all directions the roads would take them. Others clattered through the streets, firing their pistols, scaring the civilian population, all the while looting and demanding food from the townsfolk. The Rebels' fighting blood was up.

"What a horrible site!" penned 15-year-old Tillie Pierce. "There they were—human beings clad almost in rags, covered with dust, riding wildly, pell-mell down the hill toward our home shouting, yelling almost unearthly, cursing, brandishing their revolvers, and firing left and right." Local photographer Charles Tyson compared the rebels to "so many savages from the Rocky Mountains. . . ."

Rumors of Confederates had haunted the town for nearly two weeks. Eleven days prior, on June 15, a brigade of Rebel cavalry had crossed into Pennsylvania and for two days held the town of Chambersburg—25 miles to the west—hostage. After that, there were "daily, almost hourly reports of raids," wrote Gettysburg native Fannie Buehler.

"I expect to see Adams, Franklin, Cumberland, and York counties run over somewhat by the rebels," penned Boston newspaper correspondent Charles Coffin.

Once or twice, Buehler recalled, "some cavalry came as far as Cashtown and retreated. At first we were very much frightened by the thought of the Rebel soldiers invading our town. . . . As day by day passed, and they did not come, we lost faith in their coming. . . ."

The minutemen-like 26th Pennsylvania Emergency Militia had been hastily raised as first responders to the Confederate threat. They proved to be a poor response. (cm)

The Diamond today still serves as Gettysburg's town hub. (cm)

Maj. Gen. Darius Couch had been second-in-command of the Army of the Potomac at the battle of Chancellorsville. Disgusted by his commander's actions and attitude, he asked to be reassigned. His new position found him in charge of the Department of the Susquehanna, based in Harrisburg, Pennsylvania. His jurisdiction included Gettysburg. (loc)

With the entire region aflutter, Federal officials mobilized a response. On June 26, 1863, the 26th Pennsylvania Emergency Militia (PEM), stepped off their train. Led by Col. William W. Jennings, a 24-year-old combat veteran of the Army of the Potomac, the 743 men received a heroes' welcome. Primarily made up of men from central Pennsylvania, the 26th PEM was one of eight infantry militia regiments created by the Commonwealth of Pennsylvania to serve for "six months, or 'for the emergency.'" Company A consisted of Gettysburg natives.

Jennings's foot soldiers were reinforced by 45 men of Capt. Robert Bell's Adams County Cavalry Company. Twenty-three-year-old Bell had served in an independent cavalry unit the previous year, so he, like Jennings, had some military experience.

That afternoon, Maj. Granville Haller, charged with the Gettysburg area defenses, sent them all on a fool's errand: He ordered an untrained, untested militia unit to scout for, and possibly engage, the vanguard of Robert E. Lee's Army of Northern Virginia.

*   *   *

Those Confederates—a Second Corps division under Maj. Gen. Jubal Early—had come north of the Mason-Dixon line on June 22. With their eye on the Pennsylvania state capital, Harrisburg, they occupied Chambersburg en route on June 25. The next morning, June 26, amidst a rainstorm, the Confederates set out eastward toward the crossroads town of Gettysburg.

Despite the drizzle, their spirits lifted when they approached the Caledonia Furnace and Iron Works, owned by Radical Republican congressman Thaddeus Stevens. Early, a former politician himself, loathed Stevens and everything he stood for. He ordered his Rebels to burn Stevens' office, warehouse, and two forges, doling out more than $65,000 in damages.

The Confederates continued eastward. In the early afternoon, they bumped into the forward elements of the Federal militia that had deployed from Gettysburg.

The first battle of Gettysburg was about to begin.

*   *   *

Colonel Jennings had stationed 40 or so men in Gettysburg and had then set off west along the Chambersburg Pike, crossing McPherson, Herr, and Whistler Ridges. He halted the makeshift command near Marsh Creek, which acted as a natural defensive barrier, and set his men to work laying out their camp across the soggy ground. Jennings then deployed another 40 of his men and a handful of Bell's horsemen as pickets on the west side of the creek.

Receiving word of the Confederate advance, Jennings and Bell rode to the top of Whistler's ridge and realized immediately that they were no match for the Southern column marching toward them. *Strike the tents,* Jennings ordered. The colonel then told his picket line to hold as long as possible while the rest of his command withdrew.

Almost immediately, the Virginia cavalry were on the pickets with "barbarian yells and smoking pistols," one soldier said. The veteran cavaliers easily scattered the militiamen, with no loss to the Confederates.

Jennings led the bulk of his command to the northeast across wet and muddy fields. He hoped to get back to Harrisburg, and, by heading northeast, he would be able to utilize the rail line that ran east from Gettysburg. But the 17th Virginia Cavalry rode down Jennings's men and engaged them about four miles north of the town. Once more, Jennings yielded the field. The tattered remains of his unit arrived in Harrisburg two days later.

Meanwhile, back on the Chambersburg Pike, Captain Bell and his company of horsemen—perhaps 45 men—fled toward Gettysburg with White's Comanches thundering behind them. Bell called, *Every man for himself,*

Caledonia Furnace was erected in 1837 by Thaddeus Stevens, heralded by his home state as "The Great Commoner; father of the Pennsylvania common school system; the first to advocate education for the mountaineer children; early exponent of anti-slavery." The entire works, the plaque adds, were destroyed by Confederates under Jubal Early. (cm)(cm)

Erected in 1892, the monument for the 26th PEM recounts their history: "Reached Gettysburg June 25 in advance of the Army of the Potomac. On the morning of June 26 marched out the Chambersburg Pike and met the rebel column at Marsh Creek and forced by overwhelming numbers to withdraw in the afternoon. On the Hunterstown Road had a severe engagement with the rebel cavalry inflicting upon them some loss. Reached Harrisburg June 28 having marched sixty consecutive hours and skirmished with the enemy. June 30 advanced from Harrisburg after the rebels in retreat." (nps)

and his forces scattered, opening the road to the very heart of the town. In thundered the Confederates.

The first battle of Gettysburg was over.

*   *   *

Jubal Early was in a particularly onerous mood by the time he rode into the Diamond. After ensuring Jennings's rout, he turned south toward town, where he learned that some of Bell's militia had been taking potshots at White's cavalrymen. *Bushwhackers!* Early groused.

Early was a cantankerous 46-year-old Virginia native and West Point graduate who had earned the moniker "Lee's Bad Old Man." One of his subordinates, Brig. Gen. John Brown Gordon, described Early as "a bachelor, with a pungent style of commenting on things he did not like; but he had a kind heart and was always courteous to women." Not everyone saw a silver lining in the battle-tested Old Jube, though. Lee's adjutant, Col. Walter Taylor, wrote about the Bad Old Man to his fiancée: "He is a man who utterly sets at defiance all moral laws & such a one Heaven will not favour."

He had been favored on this day, though. With Gordon's infantry taking up temporary residence in the town, Early rode to the impressive courthouse and demanded a meeting with the mayor. The mayor had fled, though, leaving the president of the town council to treat with Early instead. Old Jube wrote a list of demands, which included 7,000 pounds of bacon, 1,200 pounds of sugar, 40 bushels of onions, 1,000 pounds of salt, 600 pounds of coffee, 1,000 pairs of shoes, and 500 hats; or they could simply hand over $5,000.

The town had been stripped clean, however—not by the Confederates but by the townsfolk, who had hidden their goods or shipped them off on the railroad. Town documents and mail were shipped away, too. Many of the residents themselves followed suit, some fleeing to the town of Hanover 16 miles to the east, some to the burgeoning defenses of Harrisburg to the north.

A large number of the town's free African-Americans fled, too. "I can see them yet; men and women with bundles as large as old-fashioned feather ticks slung across their backs," a witness later recalled. "The greatest consternation was depicted on all their countenances as they hurried along . . . Mothers anxious for their offspring would stop for a moment to hurry them up, saying: 'For de lod's sake, you chillen, cum right long quick! If dem rebs dun katch you dey tear you all up.'"

When it became apparent that the people of Gettysburg could not fulfill Early's supply order, Old Jube sent his butternut soldiers house to house searching for goods. This was in direct violation of General Lee's General Order No. 72, which stipulated "no private property shall be injured or destroyed by any person belonging to or connected with the army."

In the end, Early's Rebels took what they could: horses, chickens, candy, drugs, alcohol. No tons of bacon, salt, or sugar. No horde of shoes.

The next day, June 27, Early continued eastward toward York, where he confiscated more supplies before turning northward toward Harrisburg. Soon, Confederates stood on the banks of the Susquehanna, the state capital in their sights.

The Adams County Courthouse (dd)

Harrisburg rose from the east shore of the Susquehanna River as a too-tempting target. (loc)

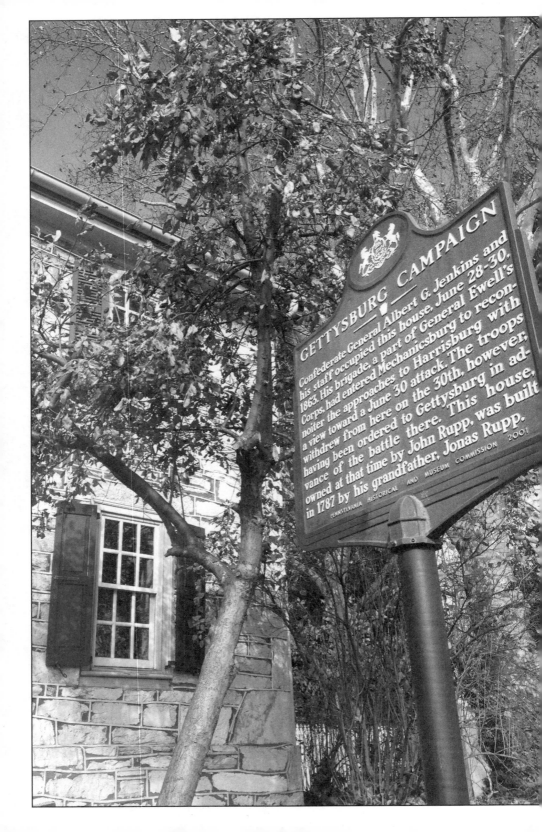

GETTYSBURG CAMPAIGN

Confederate General Albert G. Jenkins and his staff occupied this house, June 28-30, 1863. His brigade, a part of General Ewell's Corps, had entered Mechanicsburg to reconnoiter the approaches to Harrisburg with a view toward a June 30 attack. The troops withdrew from here on the 30th, however, having been ordered to Gettysburg in advance of the battle there. This house, owned at that time by John Rupp, was built in 1787 by his grandfather, Jonas Rupp.

PENNSYLVANIA HISTORICAL AND MUSEUM COMMISSION 2001

The Campaign
CHAPTER ONE
JUNE 1863

Wednesday, June 28, 1865

From Maj. Gen. George Gordon Meade, commander of the Army of the Potomac:

> *Soldiers: This day, two years [ago], I assumed command of you, under the order of the President of the Unites States. To-day, by virtue of the same authority, this army [is] ceasing to exist, I have to announce my transfer to other duties, and my separation from you.*
>
> *It is unnecessary to enumerate here all that has occurred in these two eventful years, from the grand and decisive Battle of Gettysburg, the turning point of the war, to the surrender of the Army of Northern Virginia at Appomattox Court House. Suffice it to say that history will do you justice, a grateful country will honor the living, cherish and support the disabled, and sincerely mourn the dead. . . .*

General Order No. 35 did what the Army of Northern Virginia could never do: it finished off, once and for all, the Army of the Potomac.

Meade, the army's commander, bid his men farewell in the same professional tone he had used two years earlier when he first assumed command. That June 28—1863—stood in stark contrast to the celebratory mood that buoyed the postwar country. On that former date, in the midst of an uncertain military campaign, Meade became the fourth general in eight months to command President Lincoln's principal army.

Since November 1862, the fighting men of the Army

Confederate forces reached Mechanicsburg, just a few miles from the state capital. (cm)

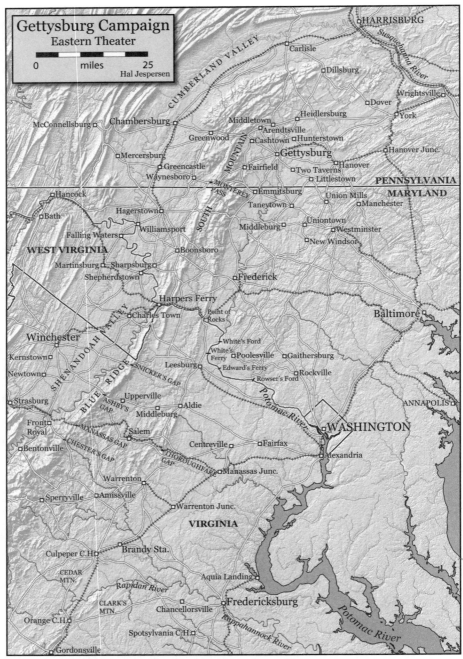

GETTYSBURG CAMPAIGN—For the first two years of the war, most of the fighting had shifted back and forth in the 100-mile corridor between Washington, D.C., and Richmond. Lee had tried to take his Confederate army northward once before, in the fall of 1862 but was turned back along Antietam Creek in Maryland. In the summer of 1863, many reasons drove Lee to decide on a second northern invasion.

The "goggle-eyed snapping turtle," Maj. Gen. George Gordon Meade (left) and "the Gray Fox," Gen. Robert E. Lee (right) (loc)

of the Potomac had endured innumerable letdowns. On November 7, their beloved commander, Maj. Gen. George B. McClellan, was relieved of command. His replacement, Maj. Gen. Ambrose E. Burnside, lasted a mere 77 days in command of the army. Mother Nature, Washington politics, and Lee's army ruined Burnside's "On to Richmond" campaign, low-lighted by the lopsided December loss at Fredericksburg.

Burnside's replacement was his arch nemesis, Maj. Gen. Joseph "Fighting Joe" Hooker. As Hooker assumed command in January of 1863, the army's morale was dangerously low. "This winter is, indeed, the Valley Forge of the war," wrote Lt. Col. Rufus Dawes of the 6th Wisconsin. But Hooker brought with him sorely needed élan and even arrogance. He reorganized the army, restored its morale, and then marched it into the Wilderness of Spotsylvania County—where he bungled a two-to-one advantage to snatch defeat from the jaws of victory at the battle of Chancellorsville.

Meade, by then commander of the Federal V Corps, watched in impotent frustration as Hooker ordered his men to give up advantages they had gained on the first day of that battle. "My God, if we can't hold the top of a hill, we certainly cannot hold the bottom of it!" he fumed. For the rest of the battle, his corps remained unengaged. After the battle, Meade's deflation was palpable: "General Hooker has disappointed all his friends by failure to show his fighting qualities at the pinch."

"Fighting Joe" Hooker first lost to Lee at Chancellorsville then picked a fight with his boss, General-in-Chief Henry Halleck. He lost that one, too —thus becoming the latest in a long string of generals to get removed from command of the Army of the Potomac. Meade would replace him. (loc)

*   *   *

The string of Federal commanders was due, in no small part, to the string of victories Gen. Robert E. Lee had amassed. After taking over Confederate forces in June, 1862, he had driven the Army of the Potomac

In the wake of the mortal wounding of Stonewall Jackson, Robert E. Lee reorganized the Army of Northern Virginia into three corps from two. Lt. Gen. James Longstreet (left) commanded the First Corps; Lt. Gen. Richard Ewell (center) commanded the Second Corps; and Lt. Gen. A. P. Hill (right) commanded the Third Corps. Lee depended heavily on Longstreet and called him "my old War Horse." Ewell and Hill had both performed exceptionally well as division commanders but remained untested at the corps level. Gettysburg would be Lee's first time employing his new command structure in battle; his learning curve would prove costly. (nps)

from the gates of Richmond in the Seven Days battles and then moved on to victory at Second Manassas. In September, he fought McClellan's much larger army to a bloody draw on the banks of Antietam Creek, and in December, he stopped Burnside cold. The victory at Chancellorsville in May of 1863 sealed his reputation.

"He sat in the full realization of all that soldiers dream of—triumph," wrote Lee's staff officer, Charles Marshall. "I thought that it must have been from such a scene that men in ancient times rose to the dignity of gods."

Chancellorsville had been a costly victory for Lee, though. Out of the nearly 60,000 Confederate soldiers engaged, 13,460 names lined the casualty rolls. Of Lee's 130 regimental commanders, 64 had been killed, wounded, or captured. The Army of Northern Virginia also lost nine general officers, and while many of them would recover from their wounds to fight another day, one important general would not: Thomas Jonathan "Stonewall" Jackson. Accidentally wounded by his own men on May 2, Jackson died of pneumonia on May 10.

Undaunted by his losses, Lee reorganized his army on May 6, and by May 14, he was in Richmond, urging Confederate President Jefferson Davis and Secretary of War James Seddon to allow him to press the war northward across the Mason-Dixon Line.

Lee hoped to accomplish many goals in pushing the war across the Potomac River. Northern Virginia had been ravaged by the hard hand of war, and by moving north, Lee planned to obtain supplies in Maryland and Pennsylvania, while his army lived off the lush countryside, thus allowing the Virginia farmers to harvest crops without the opposing army's trampling over them.

A Confederate victory on northern soil also might still attract European intervention, although the battle at

Antietam had made such intervention a long shot. By going into Pennsylvania, Lee also hoped to sow panic, discontent, and disruption throughout the North. That, in turn, might influence the fall Congressional elections.

Davis gave Lee the okay, and on June 3, the Army of Northern Virginia began what would become the most famous campaign of the war.

* * *

The weeks after Chancellorsville were arguably the darkest days of Fightin' Joe's life.

Politicians came to the army's camps and listened to the complaints of their constituents—many of them leveled at Hooker. In response, Hooker took to finger-pointing, which curdled the already sour feelings of his senior officers, who soon broke out into open revolt.

Perhaps most bruising was Hooker's diminished relationship with President Lincoln. The two had shared open, direct communication, but after Chancellorsville, Hooker was forced to communicate directly with the army's General-in-Chief, Henry W. Halleck, a longtime foe. The mutual loathing between them soon erupted into bureaucratic warfare and then escalated into a power struggle. Ever the poker player, Hooker went all in on June 27: If he could not get his way, he asked to be relieved. "You have long been aware, Mr. President, that I have not enjoyed the confidence of the major-general commanding this army," Hooker had pointed out, "and I can assure you so long as this continues, we may look in vain for success. . . ." Lincoln called Hooker's bluff and accepted his resignation.

It could not have come at a more tenuous time. By the end of June, the Army of Northern Virginia had slipped away from the banks of the Rappahannock River into the Shenandoah Valley, and Hooker's army, in cautious pursuit, was having a difficult time locating them. At Brandy Station on June 9, Confederate cavalry roughly handled their Federal counterparts after a seesaw battle. The cavalrymen then drove to within 10 miles of Washington, sending panic through the capital.

On June 15, the lead elements of Lee's army crossed the Potomac into Maryland, and on June 22 they crossed the Mason-Dixon Line into Pennsylvania. Wild rumors spread through Pittsburgh that Lee's army was driving toward the burgeoning industrial city. Fortifications were hastily erected there and in Philadelphia, and emergency regiments were quickly raised.

Confederate President Jefferson Davis (above) had been considering proposals to send a portion of the Army of Northern Virginia westward to aid the Confederate bastion at Vicksburg, Mississippi, where Union Maj. Gen. Ulysses S. Grant was engaged in a campaign to crack that stronghold wide open. Lee had proven time and again that he could do more with less, so stripping away some of his veterans for use elsewhere seemed a viable option. No one thought to reinforce *him*. Lee was, in effect, a victim of his own success: He continued to find victory despite long odds, so why did he need help? Lee countered with his invasion plan, in part, as a way to keep his army intact. His northern offensive would help Vicksburg, he reasoned, because it would tie up any blue troops in the Eastern Theater from being sent west; in fact, threatening Washington, D.C., might draw troops from the West to bolster defenses in the East. (loc)

As the armies moved northward, their cavalry clashed on several occasions. One of the first, the battle of Aldie, came on June 17, 1863, in Loudoun County, Virginia. After four hours of fighting, Federals received reinforcements, forcing the Confederates to withdraw. (loc)

By the time Hooker lost command, he had already lost control of the entire strategic picture.

* * *

Sunday, June 28, 1863, 3:00 a.m.
outside Frederick, Maryland

Colonel James Hardie had traveled all the way from Washington under special orders, arriving at George Meade's tent shortly after 3 a.m. *I've come to give you trouble,* he told the major general after entering.

Meade didn't know Hardie, but he was, indeed, expecting trouble. His relationship with Hooker, once cordial and professional, had curdled since Chancellorsville.

Through no fault of Meade's, a number of senior officers had put forward the Pennsylvanian's name as a potential replacement for the army commander.

From June 17-19, cavalry from both armies battled around Middleburg, Virginia. On June 21, they clashed again in Upperville (above). While Federal cavalry proved more aggressive than ever, their Confederate counterparts continued to effectively screen the northward movement of the army. (loc)

Typical was I Corps artillery chief Col. Charles Wainwright. "General George G. Meade was my candidate for Hooker's successor immediately after Chancellorsville, I believing him to have the longest and clearest head of any general officer in the army," he attested.

Hooker's touchy pride would not stand for it, and communications from army headquarters had grown colder and colder. Now, Meade realized, Hooker had finally decided to put him under arrest.

But Hardie offered trouble of a different sort: He bore orders promoting Meade to command of the Army of the Potomac.

Meade's ascension to command capped a wartime

Confederate cavalry made it as far north as Sterrett's Gap along Blue Mountain, just outside Carlisle Springs. A monument sits along the roadside, indicating the geographic high water mark of the Army of Northern Virginia. (cm)

GPS: N 40.28076 W 77.14866

career of stalwart service. He had quietly done his duty in the Pennsylvania Reserve Division, the I Corps, and the V Corps. At the battle of Glendale in 1862, he had been severely wounded, but he quickly returned to command and saw action as a brigade commander at Second Manassas and as a division/temporary corps commander at Antietam. At Fredericksburg, his division initially cracked the Confederate line at Prospect Hill but fell back when not reinforced. When Hooker ascended to command of the army, he promoted Meade to head the V Corps even though one of Hooker's lackeys, Brig. Gen. Daniel Butterfield, had commanded it. At Chancellorsville, Meade's men saw limited action but fought well.

An 1835 graduate of West Point, the 47-year-old Meade, balding with bags under his eyes, was known for his volcanic temper. His men called him a "god-damned goggle-eyed snapping turtle." Yet he was ever the professional soldier.

Meade carefully digested the news Hardie presented.

Confederate Brig. Gen. Albert Jenkins now has a monument, installed in the summer of 2005, outside the Rupp House, which he used as his headquarters on his march toward Harrisburg. (cm)

GPS: N 40.22385, W 76.97577

He had the unenviable task of protecting Washington and Baltimore, while at the same time locating the enemy, bringing it to battle, and defeating it as quickly as possible.

With Hardie in tow, Meade made his way through the dark early morning to Hooker's headquarters. Fighting Joe was expecting him. He briefed Meade on the disposition of the army and shared what little knowledge he had on enemy movements, then took his leave, headed for Baltimore.

Meade, meanwhile, wrote an unceremonious note to his new army. "The country looks to this army to relieve it from the devastation and disgrace of a foreign invasion. . . . I rely upon the hearty support of my companions in arms to assist me."

"General Hooker has been relieved and Gen. George G. Meade of Pennsylvania assigned to command the Army of the Potomac," wrote Rhode Island officer Elisha Hunt Rhodes. "What does it all mean?"

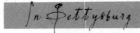

In Gettysburg

GPS: 39 49.87 N, 77 13.883 W

Many wartime structures still exist in Gettysburg, adorned with small plaques denoting their wartime pedigree. (cm)

Gettysburg's town square, with its traffic circle in the middle, is known locally as "The Diamond." As the Adams County seat, Gettysburg sat at the middle of a road network that converged from all points of the compass. Popular legend has it that Confederates first pushed into Gettysburg on June 30 because they were looking for shoes, but it was the road network, not a mythical stash of footwear, that made Gettysburg so important.

Not that there weren't shoes. Twenty-two cobblers worked in Gettysburg, says historian Gabor Boritt—a pretty standard number considering the town's population of 2,400. Had there been any inordinate surplus of shoes to take, though, Jubal Early's men would have most certainly cleaned them out on their way through on June 26, leaving scant pickings for Henry Heth.

The new county courthouse, built in 1859, was located in Gettysburg, as was the county jail, built that same year. Brick houses and gas streetlights lined the town's wide avenues. A new rail station, also built in 1859, welcomed travelers from the east; the planned extension westward had not yet been completed, although an unfinished railroad cut shot in that direction. Plans existed to take the rail line all the way to Chambersburg, a winding route that earned the project the nickname "The Tapeworm Railroad." One historian suggests a more dubious origin for the moniker "because of the way it ate up taxpayers' money."

Eight churches were scattered about town, and the Lutheran Seminary, founded in 1826, sat on the ridge along the town's northwest corner. Gettysburg also boasted a college, founded in 1832, which sat on the north edge of town. On the southern edge of town, Evergreen Cemetery, founded in 1854, topped a tall hill.

"Gettysburg," says Boritt, "was on the move, with lawyers, doctors, merchants, bankers, blacksmiths, and various craftsmen serving the surrounding countryside of small farmers. . . . Indeed, half of the population worked as artisans, a quarter as professionals, a quarter as unskilled laborers."

Boritt points out that about eight percent of the town's population—about 190 people—were free blacks; about one third of them had escaped from slavery.

Three weekly newspapers served the population, as did a number of taverns. The Gettysburg Hotel, which still operates on the northeast corner of the Diamond, offered the town's nicest lodging.

On the southeast corner of the Diamond, visitors can visit the home of David Willis. Willis, charged with establishing what became the national cemetery, invited President Lincoln to take part in the dedication ceremonies. Lincoln stayed in Willis' house during his visit.

Today, a bronze statue of Lincoln stands on the sidewalk outside the house. He lifts his stovepipe hat toward the window of the room where he once stayed, but he's looking at a sweater-wearing, tennis-shoed bronze tourist—also part of the sculpture—who looks a little bewildered. The statues are collectively called *Return Visit*.

The Gettysburg Hotel, still in operation today, first opened in 1797. (cm)

The National Park Service operates the David Willis House as a museum. (cm)

***Return Visit*, which stands in the Diamond outside the David Willis House, was sculpted by Seward Johnson, Jr. and installed in 1991.** (cm)

➡ TO STOP 2

From the Diamond, proceed west on Chambersburg Street approximately three blocks and then bear right on Buford Avenue (Route 30 West). Buford Avenue will become the Lincoln Highway. Follow Route 30 West approximately 2.5 miles. Notice Herr Tavern on the left side of the road. After passing the tavern, you will see a KOA sign on the right. Beyond the sign is a white house—the First Shot Marker is hidden on the other side of the house. There is a driveway on the house's east side that you may access, but be careful as it borders a private driveway.

GPS: 39 51.058 N, 77 16.844 W

First Shots

CHAPTER TWO

JULY 1 1863

Rumors as thick as summer humidity hung in the air of south-central Pennsylvania. Confederates had pushed their way through the mountain passes, through towns and villages, and disappeared into the countryside to the west and north, leaving behind pilfered larders and wagging tongues. Some said the Rebels now stood on the banks of the Susquehanna itself, overlooking the capital of Harrisburg. Some predicted a raid on Washington, some a raid on Philadelphia. Some wondered whether anyone could stop them.

John Buford had some ideas of his own. Some said the 37-year-old brigadier general was the best cavalryman in the Army of the Potomac, and as such, he served a vital role as the army's eyes and ears. Today, June 30, he had ridden into Gettysburg looking for Confederates.

He and his troopers had already found some earlier that morning, just eight miles to the southwest in the little village of Fairfield. "The inhabitants knew of my arrival and the position of the enemy's camp," grumbled the testy Buford, "yet none of them gave me a particle of information, not even mentioned the fact of the enemy's presence."

Townsfolk in Gettysburg, however, were more than willing to share what information they had. They were still shaken by their brush with Jubal Early's troops just four days prior. The appearance of Buford men's buoyed residents again. "It was . . . a novel and grand site," recalled one young townsperson. "I had never seen so many soldiers at one time. They were Union soldiers and that was enough for me, for I then knew we had protection, and I felt they were our dearest friends."

Buford brought 2,435 "friends" with him as part of

The first shot marker (dd)

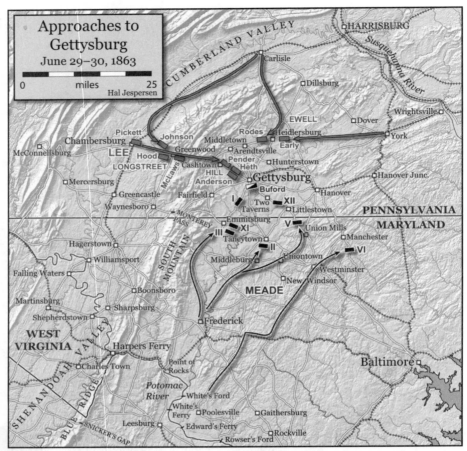

APPROACHES TO GETTYSBURG—One of the best-known "Civil War ironies" is that the Southern army approached Gettysburg from the north while the Northern army approached from the south. More accurately, the Confederate army converged on the town from the north *and* west. Neither army had a clear idea of where the other was, however. While still under Joseph Hooker, the Federal army lost track of the Confederates when they slipped away from Virginia's Rappahannock River. The Confederates, meanwhile, lost the benefit of their cavalry a few days later, which left them blind as they groped forward.

his 1st Cavalry Division. The horsemen were supported by six artillery pieces.

Buford listened as his troopers collected intelligence: Confederates had been seen lurking near Cashtown, six and a half miles to the west near the foot of the mountains. He sent Company C of the 3rd Indiana out the Chambersburg Pike to investigate.

Buford was someone "not to be trifled with," one soldier later said. A Kentucky native and 1848 graduate of West Point, Buford was "a compactly built man of middle height with a tawny moustache and a little triangular gray eye, whose expression is determined,

The view down Chambersburg Pike from McPherson's Ridge toward Herr's Ridge. (loc)

not to say sinister." He "don't put on so much style as most officers," one witness attested, appearing more like a common soldier than a brigadier general. He wore a small hat and corduroy pants that he tucked into his cowhide boots, and he carried a pipe with a large plug of tobacco.

As the Union army approached the Pennsylvania border, Buford's division was assigned to the "Left Wing" of the Army of the Potomac. Hooker had been groping for information about Confederate movements; Meade, when he replaced Fighting Joe, felt all the more blind for being thrust into command so suddenly. His cavalry *had* to get a fix on Lee's Confederates.

John Buford had just found them.

*   *   *

South-central Pennsylvania had been kind to Henry Heth, and he was looking forward to taking advantage of that kindness even more. As the vanguard of the Army of Northern Virginia, his division had found the foraging particularly good. His next significant foraging opportunity waited just to the east: the little college town of Gettysburg. Even better, it didn't appear to Heth as though there were any Federals in the area at all.

Recently promoted to major general, the 37-year-old Heth marched at the head of a column of Confederates that stretched from Cashtown back through the mountains all the way to Chambersburg: first, Lt. Gen. A. P. Hill's Third Corps, consisting of two other divisions besides Heth's, then Lt. Gen. James Longstreet's First Corps, consisting of another three divisions—more than 67,000 men in all. The rest of Lee's army, Lt. Gen. Richard Ewell's Second Corps,

John Buford's simplicity, the leather jacket he wore in the field, and his ever-present tobacco pouch covered something far greater burning inside him. The old dragoon possessed a fiery determination to not fail in any task put before him. (loc)

ν

"Discovering the Enemy" is a bas-relief sculpture on the face of the 9th New York Cavalry monument, dedicated in 1888. (cm)

In May of 1864, Maj. Gen. Henry Heth will again find himself at the lead of Hill's column, under orders not to bring on a general engagement, as he marches into the Wilderness. With the lessons of Gettysburg in mind, he will hold back from aggressive action at a time when a bold push forward would have easily swept aside a handful of Union officers who were, through sheer bluff, holding a key intersection. (loc)

had already driven north. In fact, Early's division of Ewell's Corps had passed this way just four days earlier, leaving the pickings more scant for Heth's men than Heth expected.

At around 6:30 a.m. on June 30, Heth sent three regiments from Brig. Gen. James Johnston Pettigrew's brigade to Gettysburg with orders to bring back the spoils of war.

The Tar Heel native set off. As his column moved eastward, they came upon a local doctor who told Southern officers that there were no Union soldiers in Gettysburg. Satisfied, the column pressed on.

As they crossed Wiloughby Run, though, Confederates then spotted an organized group of horsemen—a squadron of the 8th Illinois Cavalry. Pettigrew was a novice at war but was a well-educated man; he quickly surmised the situation and turned back. The shadowy horsemen followed at a safe but noticeable distance.

Later in the afternoon, Pettigrew reported what he'd found to Heth, who believed that the Army of the Potomac still lingered in Maryland. Pettigrew had seen only local scouts, Heth surmised. Nonetheless, he reported Pettigrew's findings to corps commander A. P. Hill, who agreed with Heth's assessment. *Return to Gettysburg the next morning*, Hill ordered, *and finish collecting those supplies*.

* * *

As Heth's June 30 foraging expedition unfolded, John Buford set to work. He had seen all he needed to.

The Cashtown Inn (left) was built circa 1797. The innkeeper did a cash-only business "for the entertainment of strangers and travelers," thus giving the crossroads its name. According to the inn's website, the hostelry was known for its "healthy neighborhood; pure mountain air" and "daily bath." The Inn remains in operation today (below). (achs; cm)

Setting up headquarters on Chambersburg Street at the Eagle Hotel, the veteran officer sent word to Federal Left Wing commander Maj. Gen. John F. Reynolds and cavalry commander Alfred Pleasonton: Lee's army was clearly within striking distance of Gettysburg.

Around the town itself, Buford set up a long, thin picket line of videttes—small, forward-posted groups of horsemen—covering three-quarters of Gettysburg and eight of the roads leading into the town. Behind the line of videttes, he created a number of reserve positions that could quickly send troopers to threatened points. A little farther to the rear, the bulk of Buford's troopers took position on the north and west sides of Gettysburg.

Buford planned to stall a Southern advance by taking advantage of the topography of the region—namely the numerous ridgelines of the area—and the ability of his horsemen to quickly fall back from one ridgeline to the next. From Whistler's Ridge, roughly three miles west of town, Federal troopers could fight on foot, three men battling the enemy while a fourth trooper held the others' horses. Once the rebel infantry approached too closely, the troopers would take to horse and fall back to the next ridgeline, dismount, and start anew.

That expected Southern advance came down the Chambersburg Pike early the next day, July 1.

Heth expected little more than token resistance from the scouts he'd seen the day before, but rather than send Pettigrew's untested brigade against them, he sent the veteran Alabama/Tennessee brigade of Brig. Gen. James J. Archer.

As Archer's men approached, a four-man vidette of Federal troopers spotted them. One of the Federals, Sgt. Levi Shaffer, called back to the Herr Tavern to summon the officer in the area, Lt. Marcellus Jones. Jones hurried to the front, arriving at the home of Ephraim Wisler, where his men pointed out the approaching enemy.

Herr Tavern today sits at the point where Route 30 crests Herr Ridge. (cm)

Jones asked Shaffer for his rifle.

"Give me the honor of opening this ball," he said.

Using a fence to level the rifle, the lieutenant squeezed off a round.

The battle of Gettysburg was on.

At the First Shot Marker

The First Shot Marker offers plenty of credit to go around: Fired by Capt. Jones with Sgt. Shafer's carbine, part of Co. E of the 8th Illinois Cavalry (cm)

The battle of Gettysburg began in the yard of Ephraim Wisler (sometimes spelled Whistler). Wisler was 31 years old at the time of the battle and a blacksmith by trade. His home, a two-story brick structure, was built in 1857. On the morning of July 1, Wisler, noticing activity around his house, stepped into the middle of the Chambersburg Pike for a better look. Suddenly, a Confederate shell smashed into the road near him. Though he was not hit, Wisler was nevertheless shell-shocked. He staggered back into his home, took to his bed, and died of heart failure on August 11, 1863.

Wisler's home was sold to James Mickler shortly after the Civil War. Mickler served in Bell's Adams County Cavalry Company during the June 26, 1863, battle of Marsh Creek. The home remained in private hands until 2002, when the home was purchased by the National Park Service and is now part of a 3.79-acre parcel maintained by that agency.

In the front yard of the home, which is adjacent to modern Route 30, is a small monument that was placed there in 1886 by Lieutenant Jones and his friends. It marks the approximate location of the first shot of battle, fired at 7:30 a.m. on July 1.

While standing at the monument, turn and look at the pock-marked brick on the western side of the home, which was subjected to small arms fire from the Alabamians. The Federal troopers were also subjected to Southern artillery fire.

In this area, too, fell the first casualties of the battle.

On the north side of the Chambersburg Pike, the advancing Alabamians were subjected to the fire of the 8th and 12th Illinois Cavalry, who had dismounted and were using the top rail of a fence to level their guns. The first Confederate hit was Pvt. C. F. L. Worley of Company A of the 5th Alabama Battalion, shot in the leg. On the Federal side, Pvt. John Weaver of Company A of the 3rd Indiana Cavalry was also shot in the leg. Weaver's leg was amputated, but he died on August 3, 1863, at Camp Letterman, a Union hospital established on July 22 to care for the wounded left behind after the battle. Weaver's death, delayed as it was, made him the first Federal mortally wounded during the battle.

The Confederate skirmishers were firing uphill, which meant many of their shots strayed high, scarring the west-facing wall of the Wisler home. (cm)

⟶ TO STOP 3

Turn left onto Route 30 and retrace your route toward town. Proceed 1.7 miles. You will pass Herr Tavern on the right and up ahead, also on the right, is the National Park Service Guide Station. Pull into the parking lot.

GPS: 39 83.803 N 77 25.262 W

$\mathcal{F}ight\ \mathcal{L}ike\ the\ \mathcal{D}evil$

CHAPTER THREE
JULY 1 1863

On the evening of June 30, John Buford called his brigade commanders to the Eagle Hotel. Clustered inside headquarters, they reviewed the day's events and double-checked dispositions. Buford, dressed in an old hunting jacket, puffed his pipe and listened to the reports. Two-thousand four-hundred and thirty-five cavalrymen were about to take on Lee's entire army. All they had to do was stall long enough for John Reynolds to bring up the lead elements of the Army of the Potomac.

Colonel Thomas Devin, a native New Yorker who was earning the nickname "Buford's Hard-Hitter" for his aggressive cavalry work, boasted that he could hold off any attack made against his front in the next 24 hours.

"No you won't," Buford growled. "They will attack you in the morning and will come 'booming,' skirmishers three deep. You will have to fight like the devil to hold your own until supports arrive. The enemy must know the importance of this position, and will strain every nerve to secure it, and if we are able to hold it, we shall do well."

*　　*　　*

Now, on July 1, the enemy was doing exactly as Buford predicted—and Buford's men were fighting like the devil, indeed.

Tom Devin and fellow brigade commander Col. William Gamble did all they could to hold back the enemy. They made their first stand on Herr's Ridge, the first of a series of north/sounth-running ridges. When the enemy closed too close and pressed too hard, the Federals grudgingly gave ground, falling back to the next parallel ridgeline, McPherson Ridge. "[O]ur brave boys

John Buford expected his men would have to "fight like the devil" on July 1 once Confederates came "booming." The Federals did not have to wait long. (cm)

Buford's top lieutenants: Col. Thomas Devin and Col. William Gamble (and staff). (loc)

stood firm and fell back only when ordered," an Illinois horseman remembered.

Buford set his main line of defense. Along McPherson Ridge, elements of eight Federal regiments dismounted and spread out for half a mile, with the left flank anchored on the Fairfield Road (modern day Route 116) and the right ending at the Mummasburg Road (near the modern Peace Light Memorial). Bolstering Buford's line were the six guns of Lt. John Calef's Battery A, 2nd United States Artillery.

For one of the few times in a major Eastern Theater battle, though, the Army of Northern Virginia held artillery superiority. Major William "Willie" Pegram, one of Lee's best artillerists, commanded an artillery battalion in the Confederate Third Army Corps, and he deployed 20 guns along Herr's Ridge. The Southern guns quickly dominated the open ground where Buford's men had deployed; the batteries "rained upon our men showers of shot and shell," one Union trooper wrote.

To counter the rebel threat, Buford spread out his six artillery pieces. His hope was to deceive the Confederate gunners into thinking the Federals had more cannon than he actually did.

Heth's division rolled forward toward the ridge. North of the pike was the mixed Mississippi-North Carolina brigade of Brig. Gen. Joseph Davis, nephew of Confederate President Jefferson Davis. South of the road advanced James Archer's brigade, which had opened the battle against Marcellus Jones' outpost. The two Confederate brigades numbered more than 3,200 men—fully 700 more than Buford could field— and Davis and Archer represented less than half of the manpower available to Heth.

Crossing Willoughby Run, the two brigades ascended the gentle slope, bearing down on Buford's troopers.

* * *

A quarter mile to the east, five stories above

the battlefield, John Buford stood in the cupola of Schmucker Hall, the main building of the Lutheran Theological Seminary. He watched the unfolding battle along McPherson Ridge—where the Confederates "pressed us in overwhelming numbers," his signal officer recalled—then anxiously shifted his gaze to the roads that approached Gettysburg from the south.

The cupola now atop Schmucker Hall is not Buford's original perch, although it stands in the same location. The cupola has twice been lost to fire since 1863. (cm)

The seminary cupola still offers an excellent view of McPherson's Ridge to the west. (jm)

Maj. Gen. John Reynolds looked every part the soldier. (loc)

Not until 10 a.m. did one of Buford's signal officers spy a small knot of officers riding towards them. Beyond in the distance, along the Emmittsburg Road, marched a compact column of soldiers.

"What's the matter, John?" one of the newly arrived officers called up to Buford, still in the cupola.

"The devil's to pay," Buford replied, not missing a beat. He recognized the voice: John Fulton Reynolds had arrived on the field.

The 42-year-old Pennsylvania native was a graduate of the West Point class of 1841. His Civil War career saw him as a brigade commander in the famed Pennsylvania Reserves, where he eventually rose to command the division. In 1862, he served for a time as military governor of Fredericksburg, Virginia. Later, during the Peninsula campaign, he was captured while sleeping. After he was exchanged, he more than made up for his narcolepsy with a solid performance at Second Bull Run, but at Fredericksburg, he failed to provide reinforcements that would have exploited a breakthrough at the south end of the field. Chancellorsville saw his men do far more marching than fighting, and during a council of war on the night of May 4, he ignominiously fell asleep again.

Prior to Fredericksburg, Reynolds was promoted to command I Corps, a position he held until Meade assumed the army. Meade was friends with his fellow Pennsylvanian and leaned on Reynolds not as a corps commander but rather as a wing commander, with nearly one half of Meade's available infantry under his steady hand. Thus, when Reynolds arrived at Gettysburg, he had the authority not to bring just one Federal corps of 12,222 men to the field, but to bring three infantry corps consisting of more than 32,000 infantry to the field (plus Buford's already-engaged cavalry).

Artillery emplacements today sit along McPherson's Ridge. (cm)

Reynolds had spent the previous night wrapped in a blanket, with his saddle as a pillow, sleeping on the floor of Moritz Tavern on the Emmitsburg Road, 5.8 miles south of Gettysburg. At four a.m., one of his staff officers woke him with the marching orders of the day. When he set off for the front, he passed through the camps of Brig. Gen. James Wadsworth's I Corps division. As Wadsworth's men fell into line behind Reynolds on the road to Gettysburg, a shower passed over, making the roads slippery with mud.

Now, hours later, as the mud-spattered men reached the Nicholas Codori farm just outside of town, the division was ordered off the road and across the fields leading to the Seminary grounds—double quick. In the lead marched the brigade of Brig. Gen. Lysander Cutler. Cutler had five regiments on hand, with a sixth on its way to rejoin him later (which would have haunting repercussions later).

With I Corps commander Maj. Gen. Abner Doubleday not yet on the field, Reynolds assumed personal command. He directed three of Cutler's regiments north of an unfinished railroad cut to contend with Joe Davis' Confederate brigade (an action that will be talked about in Chapter 6). He then ordered Cutler's remaining two regiments forward along the south side of the Chambersburg Pike to contend with Archer.

To bolster Cutler's line and relieve Calef's battered artillerymen, Reynolds threw forward his only other battery on hand, Capt. James Hall's 2nd Maine Artillery. Hall and I Corps Chief of Artillery Col. Charles S. Wainwright were none too pleased with the deployment. "I did not like this advanced position at all," recalled Wainwright, complaining of the battery's "right flank being exposed to a high ridge to the north, and approached by a number of ravines which afforded excellent cover to an attacking party."

Despite Confederate pressure, Hall's gunners stood

Brig. Gen. Lysander Cutler was a hardnosed Massachusetts man. One of his soldiers described him as being "rugged as a wolf." (loc)

One of the more colorful units in the army were the Pennsylvania Bucktails. The men of the brigade wore deer tails on their hats to demonstrate their prowess as marksmen. The original regiment, the 42nd Pennsylvania, was raised from the woodland mountains of northwestern Pennsylvania, and their sharpshooting was so impressive early in the war that a second group of Bucktails was recruited. Those regiments, the 149th and 150th Pennsylvania Infantry, were initially derided as the "Bogus Bucktails," but on July 1, they earned their mettle. Thrown into battle, they vowed, "We're here to stay," which eventually became their motto. When Confederates resumed their attacks in the early afternoon, the Bucktails sutained fire from two directions, yet they held off an attack by Junius Daniel's North Carolina brigade. In doing so, though, the Bucktails sustained 853 casualties—or 64.8%. (cm)

to their work. "The flank attack was made directly upon Hall's battery," one observer later recalled, "and though he was successful in checking it . . . he was obliged to leave one piece on the field, all six of the horses being shot down as they stood."

Cutler's timely arrival and Hall's stalwart stand—all directed by Reynolds—momentarily stemmed the Confederate advance. But even as more Federals filed onto the field, more Rebels funneled down the Chambersburg Pike.

The devil was, indeed, to pay because all hell had broken loose.

At the Buford / Reynolds Monuments

The McPherson farmstead included a large barn, home, wagon house, and other various outbuildings. (gnmp)

One of the main fixtures on the July 1 battlefield is the farmstead of Edward M. McPherson, a former Republican Congressman who had served from 1859 through March of 1863. At the time of the battle, McPherson was in Washington, D.C., serving as a deputy commissioner for Internal Revenue. While McPherson was away, he rented the home to John Slentz. Slentz took his wife and five children from the home as the battle opened and spent the next few days taking refuge in the home of Harvey Sweeny along Baltimore Street.

As the action of the first day swirled around the farm, the barn was used to house riflemen of the Pennsylvania

Battle damage scarred the exterior of the McPherson barn during the battle; the agony of the wounded haunted it after. (loc)

Bucktail brigade, who used the ventilation slits on the north side of the barn to fire at oncoming Confederates.

After the battle, McPherson's barn was used as a field hospital. Local attorney William McClean, who visited the barn, wrote an account:

> *I was informed that the men were suffering in the McPherson barn. . . . My good wife went to work, baked biscuit, prepared gruel, and we gathered fresh Antwerp raspberries . . . and loaded up with as much as I could carry. . . . When I entered the barn it was crowded with the wounded of both armies, some of them fallen four days before and without having any food, except in some cases the little hardtack in their haversacks, and without surgical attention to their wounds. There was so many of these wounded and so closely packed together, that I was obliged to tramp on some of them in distributing my supplies. . . . Many of these poor fellows must have died afterwards from gangrene.*

By early August, the wounded were evacuated to Camp Letterman, a massive field hospital a few miles to the east of town. The battle had so ravaged the farm, though, that it took more than three months to repair

The Buford and Reynolds monuments along the Chambersburg Pike, looking toward Gettysburg. (loc)

the damage to the buildings. During that time, the Slentz family lived in Schmucker Hall at the Lutheran Theological Seminary.

The home and outbuildings survived the war, but in 1895 the house was consumed in a fire. All that remains of the farm now is the barn, which was restored in 1978 by the National Park Service.

The cluster of monuments on the western edge of the park along Route 30 pays tribute to two of the most famous generals to fight at Gettysburg.

The large equestrian statue depicts John Reynolds. Dedicated on July 1, 1899—the 36th anniversary of the battle—the statue was designed by Henry Kirke Bush-Browne at the cost of $27,666.

The Reynolds monument in the national cemetery was the first bronze statue erected at Gettysburg. It was cast from the tubes of four bronze cannons. (cm)

The large Reynolds statue is not the only monument on the field to the famed Pennsylvania general. The oldest Reynolds monument sits near the Baltimore Pike entrance inside of Soldiers' National Cemetery (a.k.a. Gettysburg National Cemetery). It was dedicated on August 31, 1872.

A third Reynolds monument sits at the edge of Herbst Woods, memorializing the area where Reynolds fell; it was dedicated on the twenty-third anniversary of the general's death.

Standing near Reynolds's equestrian statue, peering to the west, is a statue of John Buford. When the monument was dedicated on July 1, 1895, a good bit of controversy swirled around the monument's design. Sculptor James Kelly decided not to place the famed cavalryman on horseback; rather, Kelly depicted Buford dismounted in the same fashion that his troopers had fought on July 1. It was "suggested that it would be better for me to stay home and not attend the unveiling," Kelly remembered. The monument committee, including cavalry Gen. James H. Wilson, were set against Kelly's depiction of Buford—until they actually saw the monument. Wilson, once an outspoken critic of the monument, became Kelly's "most devoted friend." Former Buford classmate John Tiball exclaimed, "I knew Buford at West Point, served with him in the Mexican War, and saw him at Gettysburg. The proportions are good—the character is good. That's Buford!"

Around the base of the Buford monument are four of the six cannon deployed by Calef's Battery at Gettysburg. The first shot fired by a Federal artillery piece came from these cannon—specifically gun number 233, which was forged at the Phoenixville Iron Works in Phoenixville, Pennsylvania. Calef, who survived the

The epitome of the American military is the citizen soldier, taking up arms to defend hearth, home, and country. Gettysburg resident John Burns (above, right) personified this image. On July 1, the elderly veteran of the War of 1812 picked up his flintlock rifle and powder horn and told his wife he wanted "to see what was going on." He spent the day fighting alongside several Union regiments, including those in the Iron Brigade. He was wounded three times. Burns survived the battle and met President Abraham Lincoln prior to the dedication of the Soldier's Cemetery. Burns would be immortalized in a Bret Harte poem as the man "who held his own in the fight next day, when all the townfolk ran away." On July 1, 1903, he was further immortalized when Pennsylvania dedicated a bronze statue to him along Stone Avenue (above, left). (loc)(loc)

war, actually tracked down the four cannon that had also survived. At the dedication of the monument, Calef spiked the gun so that "it may speak no more."

A brass plate on cannon 233 makes it easy to identify as "the opening gun of the battle." (cm)

→ **TO STOP 4**

Pull out of the parking lot and bear immediately to the right onto Stone-Meredith Avenue. Follow the road to the edge of the woods. On the way, note the McPherson Barn and the statue to John Burns. Once the road begins to curve downhill, there is ample parking on the right side.

GPS: 39 50.133 N, 77 15.241 W

Herbst Woods

CHAPTER FOUR

JULY 1 1863

As the vanguard Confederate unit, James Archer's brigade had a particularly tough go of it with the Federal cavalry. The horsemen mounted and dismounted at will, forcing Archer's men to engage and disengage time and time again. The exchange ultimately resulted in a net gain of real estate for the Confederates but at the cost of a lot of time and organization.

Archer was a brave and tough commander. A graduate of Princeton University, he had been commissioned as a captain during the Mexican-American War. Afterwards, he left the army for a short time, but returned in 1855. As a native of Baltimore, he threw his hat in the ring with the Confederacy when civil war broke out. Although he was a Marylander, he commanded a mixed brigade of Tennessee and Alabama forces. The men had performed well at Second Manassas, Antietam, and Chancellorsville.

By 10:30 a.m., Archer's entire brigade had deployed into line of battle, moving from Herr's Ridge toward McPherson Ridge. Rather than press along the open ridgeline toward the McPherson Barn, though, where Federal artillery was posted, Archer's brigade bore down on a woodlot a little to the south—Herbst Woods, owned by farmer John Herbst, whose home sat 750 yards to the southwest. Federal sharpshooters took up residence in his barn, which Confederates later torched. Archer hoped to flank the Federal artillery while disposing of Buford's pesky troopers, using the woodlot for cover.

Gamble's men, opposing Archer's, hotly contested the Confederate approach. "We continued to advance, but in a walk," wrote Pvt. William H. Moon of the 13th Tennessee, "loading and firing as we went, until we reached a strip of low land along the Run. There we were protected from the fire of the enemy by an abrupt

John Gibbon's Iron Brigade had become known as the "Black Hats" because of the distinctive high, black Hardee hats each man wore. They became such a part of the brigade's identity that one of the regiments, the 2nd Wisconsin, included one on its monument. (cm)

The woodlot known as McPherson's Woods was not actually on McPherson's Ridge. That woodlot was called Herbst Woods (right). McPherson's Woods sat on the same ridgeline as the Seminary, a little to the east, near an unfinished railroad cut. (loc)

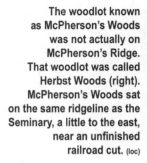

James Archer had earned the nickname "The Little Gamecock" for his scrappiness, although by nature he was a frail and sickly man who normally fell ill before every battle he entered—yet he never stayed in his sickbed when battle was eminent. (loc)

rise across the Run in our front. We halted to reform, reload, catch our breath, and cool off a little."

Archer's men pushed up from the banks of Willoughby's Run, aiming toward the woodlot. They made it about 75 yards when the entire tactical situation instantly changed. Elements of Cutler's brigade arrived, flooding the woodlot with fresh Federal reinforcements.

Slowing Archer was not enough, though—but that was all Cutler's men could do. So, Reynolds turned to his last available brigade, which was even then pouring through the fields from the Lutheran Theological Seminary: the famed "Iron Brigade," consisting of five regiments from Wisconsin, Michigan, and Indiana.

The Iron Brigade was one of the finest units in either army at Gettysburg. Their first major action as a brigade was at Brawner's farm—the opening action at Second Manassas—but the 2nd Wisconsin Infantry had served in the army since First Manassas, where they actually wore gray uniforms. At the September 1862 battle of South Mountain, the brigade earned their now well-known nickname when Maj. Gen. George B. McClellan said, "They must be made of iron."

First arriving in the vicinity of the Seminary, the Westerners were directed across the fields leading to the McPherson farm and Herbst Woods. Most of the Federal units did not expect to be thrown into the battle so quickly. Only one regiment carried loaded rifles, the 19th Indiana, which had served on picket duty the evening before. Men in the rest of the brigade loaded at will as they marched toward the fray. The 24th Michigan attempted to halt and load, but they were ordered "to move forward immediately without loading" by a staff officer who sensed the urgency of the situation.

The men took fire as they moved across the fields into battle. The 19th Indiana's color bearer was hit by a dozen bullets; by the end of the day, the regiment would lose seven more. The colonel and lieutenant colonel of the 2nd Wisconsin both fell. So, too, did John Reynolds (whose death will be discussed in the next chapter).

But the exhaustion of chasing cavalry and now the overwhelming numbers of the Iron Brigade finally proved to be too much for Archer's men. The killing blow came when the 24th Michigan found Archer's left flank and began to engulf it. The Southerners fled back toward Herr's Ridge.

On the brigade's right, the situation got even worse. "Here we were, surrounded nearly on all sides," read an August 1863 article in the *Richmond Enquirer*, "but our brave little Brigadier [Archer] ordered his men to fight to the last, and never did one of the Brigade surrender until the enemy was within ten to fifteen paces of the General." Trying to stem the disaster, Archer was captured near a stone quarry on the northwest side of the woodlot.

Archer's brigade was effectively out of the fight for the remainder of the morning.

Willoughby Run is one of several small streams that surround Gettysburg. (cm)

At Herbst Woods

For the most part, the topography of the ridge where the McPherson farm sat was open and rolling, but Herbst Woods, as the exception, serves as an excellent example of the numerous woodlots that dotted the Gettysburg landscape in 1863. Unlike the choking woods of Chickamauga or the Wilderness—whose many grape vines, scrub oaks, and jagger bushes made the forest floor nearly impassable—the numerous Gettysburg woodlots were relatively well tended. Farmers allowed their animals—cows, pigs, horses, and even chickens—to roam through the lots and graze there freely. This kept the undergrowth at a minimum. Farmers also utilized selective cutting of trees for fencing, firewood, and other daily necessities. Such practices made the woodlots open enough that troops could pass through easily, while also having a relatively unobscured line of sight. Thus, many of the woods around Gettysburg gave both Union and Confederate troops cover, while not overtly hindering the mobility of the units within.

"[H]ere are those damned black hat fellows again," one North Carolinian said of the Iron Brigade as the two units slugged it out in Herbst Woods. Their grim contest took a heavy toll on both sides. (cm)

When the Iron Brigade engulfed the flanks of Archer's brigade—due to a gap between Archer's and Davis' brigades—Archer was on foot, trying to shore up his men. He was captured and taken into custody by Pvt. Patrick Maloney of the 2nd Wisconsin. Maloney was apparently a madman when he captured the general, for when Archer was presented to Lt. Dennis Dailey, Archer asked Dailey to protect him from the private. Dailey took the general's sword and sent Archer on to I Corps commander Maj. Gen. Abner Doubleday. Doubleday, who knew Archer, smiled and said, "I am glad to see you!" The angry little gamecock cawed back: "Well, I am not glad to see you by a damned sight." Archer was the first general officer to be captured in battle since Lee had taken over the Army of Northern Virginia on June 1, 1862.

Dailey and Maloney, meanwhile, both went on to fight that afternoon against Pettigrew's North Carolina Brigade. Dailey was wounded in the battle and taken to the home of Mary McAllister, whom he entrusted with the sword. Days later, after the battle ended, Dailey came to find out that Col. Henry Morrow of the 24th Michigan had taken the sword from the McAllister home as a prize. Morrow later returned the sword to Dailey, who did not

keep it, but gave it to his brigade commander, Brig. Gen. Solomon Meredith, as a gift. Upon Meredith's death in 1881, the sword was returned to the lieutenant.

Maloney did not fare as well as Dailey. That afternoon, Maloney was killed in action. He was posthumously awarded the Medal of Honor for his actions at Gettysburg.

The 24th Michigan lost more men killed or wounded than any other regiment at Gettysburg. According to another of the regiment's markers, located on Culp's Hill, "Of the 496 men who went into battle on July 1, 1863, 99 answered roll call here on the morning of July 2. . . ." (cm)

⟶ TO STOP 5

Continue around the large bend in Stone-Meredith Avenue. As the road straightens, you will see a stop sign ahead at the intersection of Stone-Meredith Avenue and Reynolds Avenue South. At the stop sign, turn left. There is ample parking ahead on the right. Opposite, there will be a lone monument marking the spot where Maj. Gen. John Reynolds fell. Get out of your car and walk back to the monument.

GPS: 39 50.079 N, 77 15.021 W

The Death of John Reynolds

CHAPTER FIVE

JULY 1 1863

"Forward, men!" John Reynolds cried out to the 2nd Wisconsin as they drove toward Archer's butternut brigade. "Forward, for God's sake, and drive those fellows out of those woods!"

Reynolds spared a glance toward the rear. Reinforcements should be arriving any minute, or so he hoped. As the battle opened, he had sent his aide, Capt. Stephen Weld, rushing back to Meade's headquarters in Taneytown, Maryland, some 13 miles from the field. Weld arrived at 11:20 a.m. with Reynolds's message: *I've made contact with the Confederates*, Reynolds told Meade, and "the enemy were coming on in strong force, and that he was afraid they would get the heights on the other side [south side] of the town. . . ." Reynolds vowed to "fight them all through the town . . . and keep them back as long as possible."

Meade had to get the rest of the army up.

Reynolds glanced again rearward. More of his own men were quick-timing across the rolling fields from Seminary Ridge—the next regiments of the Iron Brigade. No other elements of the army, though.

Suddenly Reynolds slumped—then he slid from his saddle.

"When he fell we sprang from our horses," recalled Sgt. Charles Veil. "[T]he Gen'l. fell on his left side, I turned him on his back, glanced over him but could see no wound escept a bruise above his left eye. We were under the impression that he was only stunned, this was all done in a glance. I caught the Genl. under the arms, while each of the Capt's. took hold of his legs, and we commenced to carry him out of the woods towards the Seminary."

"I cannot realize that he is dead," said one Union officer after seeing John Reynolds carried to the rear in an ambulance. "The last time I saw him he was alive and well, and now to think of him as dead seems an impossibility." (cm)

One of several sketches artist Alfred Waud did of the death of Reynolds. (loc)

Reynolds was not just stunned: he was dead. "[A] Minnie Ball Struck him in the back of the neck, and he fell from his horse dead," revealed Veil. "He never spoke a word, or moved, a muscle after he was struck. I have seen many men killed in action, but never saw a ball do its work so <u>instantly</u> as did the ball which struck General Reynolds. . . ."

* * *

With Reynolds dead, command of the field temporarily fell to Maj. Gen. Abner Doubleday, who later admitted he was a little "overwhelmed" by the situation. Doubleday had long served in the I Corps and knew the men and officers well, but on July 1, he was only just getting used to serving as temporary corps commander due to Reynolds' elevation to wing commander.

Once believed to be the inventor of baseball, it now seems obligatory for Civil War texts to point out that Maj. Gen. Abner Doubleday did *not* invent the sport. (loc)

Doubleday, the reputed creator of baseball (though not true), was a New York state native who had just celebrated his 44th birthday on June 26. He was a West Point graduate of the class of 1842—one year behind Reynolds—where he ranked 24 out of 56 cadets. In April 1861, Doubleday commanded and sited the first Federal gun to return Confederate fire at Fort Sumter. He rose through the ranks, eventually heading a brigade in the Army of Virginia and, later, a division in the Army of the Potomac's I Corps.

Doubleday was a brave soldier, but he had a habit of rubbing most people the wrong way—a trait that would soon surface in spades with the Army of the Potomac's new commander. Yet, after the fall of Reynolds, Doubleday performed admirably on his own, with very little guidance from higher headquarters.

Doubleday sent word about Reynolds to Meade. Word also reached the next ranking officer in the chain of command, Maj. Gen. Oliver O. Howard, commander of the XI Corps, who had been ordered up to Gettysburg just before Reynolds's death. The Maine native dashed off toward Gettysburg to assume Reynolds's role as left wing commander.

The death of Reynolds came as a shock to Meade. A staff officer recalled that Meade's expression took on one of grim sadness when he received the news. The fellow Pennsylvanian had been a good friend and trusted advisor—both so necessary to the new army commander as he still tried to find his feet.

To make matters worse—far worse, as far as Meade was concerned—the three commanders closest to the field were Doubleday, a man Meade loathed; Howard, one of the men responsible for the Federal defeat at Chancellorsville two months earlier; and III Corps commander Daniel Sickles, a non-West Point grad and loose cannon. This was not the A-list team of generals the Army of the Potomac needed at the front.

Meade made the prudent decision to dispatch Maj. Gen. Winfield S. Hancock to the front. Like Meade and Reynolds, Hancock was a native Pennsylvanian and a West Point graduate. He had fought well on the Peninsula and at Fredericksburg and Chancellorsville. In May of 1863, Hancock had been slated to assume command of Hooker's Cavalry Corps, but Darius Couch's demands for reassignment opened the leadership of the II Corps, and Hancock was assigned there instead.

Named after one of America's most famous military heroes, Winfield Scott, the former chief of the U.S. army, Maj. Gen. Winfield Scott Hancock seemed almost destined for military greatness. It's little wonder that by July of 1863, his fighting record had earned him the *nom de guerre* "Hancock the Superb." (loc)

Hancock was junior to Doubleday and Howard, but he was a solid commander Meade could trust. He was also a commander that Buford and many others would have been acquainted with. In fact, it may even have been a message from Buford that influenced Meade to send Hancock in the first place: "For God's sake send up Hancock."

Hancock, Meade knew, would do what was best for the army and rectify the muddled chain of command until Meade himself could arrive on the scene.

Still, it would take several more hours for Hancock to get there—and more Confederates were about to get there first.

At the Spot Where Reynolds was Shot

On the eastern side of Herbst Woods, a tree-shaded monument marks the approximate location where John Reynolds died.

Reynolds was a native of Lancaster, Pennsylvania, a town 55 miles east of Gettysburg. Returning his body home for burial turned out to be quite a feat, though, since Confederate cavalry prowled the lands in between. Reynolds' staff extracted the general's body from Herbst Woods, but were initially unable to find where the bullet had hit him. Finally they found the small wound in the back of Reynolds's neck. Dr. John T. Stillman, surgeon of the 147th New York, examined the body and declared Reynolds dead.

Reynolds's body was taken to the George George house (that is not a typo) at the south edge of Gettysburg. There, orderlies placed it in a crate. They had to knock one end out of it, though, in order to make the body fit. The makeshift casket made its way past army headquarters at Taneytown and then was placed on a train at Westminster, Maryland, and taken to Baltimore, where the body was embalmed and placed in a proper casket. From Baltimore, the body was taken via rail to Philadelphia and, finally, to Lancaster—a total trip of some 240 miles to cover the 55-mile distance. John Reynolds was buried on July 4, 1863.

"The place where Gen. Reynolds was killed" was originally marked by a simple hand-painted board tacked to a tree. (loc)

John Reynolds was the highest-ranking officer to fall at the battle of Gettysburg, but many people are surprised to discover that he was not the highest-ranking officer to fall in the Union army. That unfortunate distinction belongs to Maj. Gen. John Sedgwick, commander of the VI Corps, who was killed by a sharpshooter on May 9, 1964, at the battle of Spotsylvania Court House. Reynolds is not even second on the list. That was Maj. Gen. James B. McPherson, commander of the Army of the Tennessee, killed in Atlanta on July 22, 1864. Reynolds appears on the list at number three.

Also within yards of Reynolds' death site stands a monument to his temporary successor, Abner Doubleday. Doubleday's tenure as I Corps commander was short lived. After the Union army fell back to the hills and ridges south of Gettysburg late on July 1, the I

Corps took much of the blame for the fall of the Union position north and west of town. Those unfair accusations came largely from acting wing commander Oliver Otis Howard—who had, himself, taken heaps of blame for collapsing at Chancellorsville two months prior. In order to deflect blame from the collapse of his XI Corps at Gettysburg, the pot took to calling the kettle black, directing Meade's attention to the I Corps instead. It was all Meade needed to hear since he had little use for Doubleday to begin with. On July 2, Doubleday was demoted back to the division level, and Maj. Gen. John Newton was transferred in from the VI Corps to assume leadership of Reynolds's former command. Four days after the battle, Doubleday asked to be relieved, never to serve with the Army of the Potomac again.

Dedicated on September 25, 1917, the Abner Doubleday monument memorializes the often-overlooked general. (cm)

➤ TO STOP 6

Drive straight on Reynolds Avenue South to the stoplight at the intersection with Route 30. Proceed straight through the intersection onto Reynolds Avenue North. Ahead you will cross the bridge that spans the Gettysburg Railroad Cut. After crossing the bridge, pull over and park on the right.

GPS: 39 50.294 N, 77 14.864 W

The Railroad Cut

CHAPTER SIX

JULY 1 1863

"Hold the attention of the enemy until the infantry gets into position," John Reynolds had told artillery Capt. James Hall before his death. Following Reynolds' direction, Hall grudgingly plugged the 2nd Maine Artillery into place south of the Chambersburg Pike and prepared a desperate defense to buy time.

To support the artillery, Lysander Cutler's men streamed onto the field. Three of Cutler's regiments were dispatched across an unfinished railroad cut and ordered to fill in on the battery's right. Colonel John William Hofmann's veteran 56th Pennsylvanians were the first Federals to deploy across the cut.

Through the wheatfield in front of him, the 39-year-old colonel spied a compact group of soldiers driving towards his command. He turned to Cutler, who had accompanied the Pennsylvanians to their assigned position. "Is that the enemy?" Hofmann asked.

"Yes," Cutler replied.

That was all Hofmann needed to hear. "Ready! Right Oblique Aim! Fire!" he bellowed. Hofmann's men unleashed the first Federal infantry volley of the battle.

But they had picked a fight the Confederates were ready for.

* * *

The oncoming Confederates—Joseph R. Davis's brigade—was a behemoth compared to Cutler's undersized regiments. Two of the units, the 42nd Mississippi and the 55th North Carolina, were seeing their first true taste of combat.

The Tar Heels were downhill, at a range of about 500 yards, when Hofmann unloaded on them. Although

The unfinished railroad cut has long since been finished.
(cm)

With charges of nepotism swirling around him, Joseph R. Davis—Jefferson Davis's nephew—was commissioned a brigadier general on September 15, 1862. He would survive the war and live another 31 years, dying on September 15, 1896. (loc)

two members of the 55th's color guard were hit, the volley gave their colonel, John Connally, a better idea of what he was up against. He realized that he outnumbered—and outflanked—his enemy, so he began to wheel his regiment to the right for a better angle of attack.

More Federal reinforcements arrived: the 76th New York, which swung into place to the right of the Pennsylvanians. Their major, Andrew Grover, didn't realize that the North Carolinians were now coming right for that same spot. The New Yorkers began taking volleys from the Tar Heels and even from some of the Mississippians.

Even though Connally now faced the combined firepower of two Federal regiments, his single regiment of North Carolinians still outnumbered them both—640 to 627. Perhaps an even more powerful motivation than numbers drove him: as the only non-Mississippi unit in Davis' brigade, a rivalry had developed between his North Carolinians and Davis' other regiments. Connally wanted his men to be first to break the Federal line.

Federals kept up their fire from the high ground. Bullets ripped through Connally's left arm and right hip. His second in command, Maj. Alfred Belo, rushed to the colonel's side. "Pay no attention to me!" Connally admonished. "Take the colors and keep ahead of the Mississippians."

James Wadsworth's statue, which stands north of the railroad cut, was dedicated on October 6, 1914. (cm)

Belo followed his commander's advice and drove in the flank of the 76th New York. Their colonel was killed in the onslaught, and his men—outnumbered, outflanked, and out gunned—wisely made for the rear.

But just as the North Carolinans were driving their attack home, a new Federal regiment arrived on the north side of the railroad cut. The 147th New York, known as the "Oswego Regiment," was commanded by Lt. Col. Francis Miller. They anchored their left flank on the railroad cut, but their right flank was in the air because they came into position 150 yards *in front* of the other Federal units. That immediately entangled them in a fight with both regiments of Mississippians. Outnumbered three to one, members of the Oswego Regiment "were falling like autumn leaves," one observer said; "the air was full of lead."

Federal Brig. Gen. James Wadsworth saw the impending crisis and dispatched orders for his New Yorkers to retreat. Miller received the message but, just as he turned to order his men out, he was shot in the head. His horse carried his body to the rear.

Miller's second in command, Maj. George Harney, unaware of the order to withdraw, stood to his guns. In the fight, the color bearer of the regiment, Sgt. John Hinchcliff, "a Swede, six feet two, fair haired, blue eyed," went down; Sgt. William Wybourn extracted the flag from under him.

Noticing that the New Yorkers still were still fighting despite his order to withdraw, Wadsworth sent another staff officer to order them out. This time, Harney received the word. "In retreat, double-quick, run!" he ordered.

Some of Harney's men escaped back to Oak Ridge where survivors from Cutler's other two roughly handled regiments had begun to reform.

Others clambered down into the cut and, using it for cover, tried to make their way back towards the town. Confederates easily trapped them there by "throw[ing] up a barricade of rails" farther down the cut, a survivor said. "Many of our men perished before they could get out." Others climbed up the rocky face of the cut and made their way to safety.

As Sergeant Wybourn made for safety with the recovered flag of the 147th, he "received a shot, and fell on the colors as if dead." A lieutenant tried to remove the flag from the apparently dead sergeant, who would not let it go. *Relinquish the flag*, the lieutenant ordered. "Hold on," Wybourn said, "I will be up in a minute." Then, according to one witness, he "rolled over and staggered to his feet and carried them all through the fight. . . ."

Survivors of the regiment streaming to the rear passed Cutler, who was clearly angry from being bested by Joe Davis' men. "You have lost your colors, sir," Cutler growled at Major Harney.

Proudly, Harney pointed toward Wybourn, who

Organized in late September of 1862, the 147th New York had yet to see combat, but disease had severely diminished their numbers. They brought only 380 men to the field and lost 296 of them—78% of the men engaged. (cm)

was just then struggling to get off the field. "General," Harney declared, "the 147th never loses its colors."

"I take it all back," Cutler replied. "It was just like cock-fighting today. We fight a little and run a little. There are no supports."

Luckily for Cutler, he was wrong: support was on its way.

* * *

As Joe Davis' brigade had its way with Cutler's men and drove them from the railroad cut, they also drove off James Hall's artillery, which had fought "for dear life" before escaping, one Mainer said. During the fight, Confederates had repositioned so that they now faced south. "[I]n changing front the men were all tangled and confused," recalled one sergeant.

More Federals arrived on the field. In their confusion, Davis' men thought the best way to meet them was to dive into the railroad cut they had just driven the New Yorkers from and use it as a readymade trench. Confederates had done the same thing at Second Manassas the previous August, using an unfinished cut to tremendous effect; in theory, this cut offered the same sort of opportunity.

In practice, though, the choice would turn out to be a disaster. "Our men

The unfinished railroad cut (loc)

thought [the cut] would prove a good breastwork," one Confederate said, "but [the side] was too steep. . . ."

While the 42nd and 2nd Mississippi dove into the cut, the bulk of the North Carolinians remained out of the cut on its north side. With all three units intermingling, and all three regimental commanders' casualties, unit cohesion was gone. They were, said one Mississippi officer, "jumbled together without regiment or company." Thinking that discretion the better part of valor, Davis ordered his disorganized hoard off the field and back to Herr Ridge.

But it was too late. Doubleday saw the opportunity and seized it. He was in control of the field and not missing a beat.

Doubleday had one regiment left as a reserve, and he threw it in: the 6th Wisconsin, led by Lt. Col. Rufus

Dawes. Also attached was the brigade guard—20 men from each regiment of the Iron Brigade, totaling two additional officers and 100 enlisted men, who could be used for various fatigue duties. Dawes split the guard in two, placing one company and one officer on each of his flanks. "Go like hell!" a staff officer told the men.

Halfway to their objective, the 6th Wisconsin shook out into a line of battle. From his vantage point on horseback, Dawes made out Cutler's men in full retreat. Suddenly Dawes' horse was hit, carrying the young officer to the ground. In an instant, though, he popped to his feet. His men met him with a cheer.

"The regiment halted at the fence along the Cashtown [Chambersburg] Turnpike, and I gave the order to fire," he recounted. "In the field, beyond the turnpike, a long irregular line of yelling Confederates could be seen running forward and firing, and our troops were running back in disorder. The fire of our carefully aimed muskets, resting on the fence rails, striking their flank, checked the rebels in their headlong advance."

To keep up a steady stream of fire, Dawes ordered the men to "fire by file." Any Rebels still in pursuit of Cutler's regiments now turned to meet the new threat and dove in the "earthwork" in front of them. The move caught Dawes by surprise, he admitted, because he "was not aware of the existence of a railroad cut."

Lt. Col. Rufus Dawes was just three days shy of his 25th birthday when he led his Wisconsin men into the fight by the railroad cut. (loc)

Alfred Waud sketched the fight in the railroad cut. (loc)

As the two sides blazed away at each other, Dawes decided to break the impasse by ordering the 6th over the fence and at the enemy. Other regiments arrived to help. At about that same time, Confederates received orders from Joe Davis to pull back to Herr Ridge.

On the south lip of the cut, the color bearer of the 2nd Mississippi, William Murphy, planted the regimental flag to taunt the oncoming Yankees. Federals fell for the bait. Lieutenant William Remington rushed for the rebel colors and was hit twice in the effort. "I crawled forward, got up, walked backward until I got through our regiment, spoke to Major [John F.] Hauser, got damned for going after the flag and started for the rear on my best run," he later lamented. "Flag taking was pretty well knocked out of me."

Among the other groups of men who went for Murphy's flag was Ohio native Cpl. Francis A. Waller. "[A] large man made a rush for me and the flag," Murphy recalled. "As I tore the flag from the staff he took hold of me and the color." Finally, the Yankee corporal came out with the flag, "threw it down and loaded and fired twice

A popular lithograph depicted the fight in the railroad cut surrounded by ornamental flags, including flags bearing corps insignia. Ironically, the cut was the scene of many capture-the-flag struggles. (loc)

[while] standing on it. While standing on it there was a 14th Brooklyn man took hold of it and tried to get it, and I had threatened to shoot him before he would stop."

Waller eventually gave the flag to Dawes, who in turn tied it around the waist of Sgt. William Evans, who had been wounded and had hobbled to the rear using two rifles as crutches. Evans made it to the Jacob Hollinger's home on the east side of town where he initially received care. When the town fell to the Confederates, Evans hid the flag in the mattress he was laying on. Evans survived his Gettysburg wound and returned the flag to Dawes, who forwarded it on to General Meade as prize of battle. For his actions in seizing the flag, Waller received the Medal of Honor.

By 11 a.m., the fighting along McPherson Ridge petered out.

*   *   *

While John Buford had recognized the strength of the topography, the Army of the Potomac also enjoyed another significant benefit early on July 1—one that Buford, or any Federal officer, could not have anticipated: No high-ranking Confederate officer seemed to want to take control of the fight.

Division commander Henry Heth had started the battle of Gettysburg, which was growing from a minor skirmisher to a pitched battle—something Robert E. Lee wanted to avoid until his army had fully concentrated. Heth committed only two brigades and a battalion of artillery at a time when bolder action could have actually avoided a pitched battle by completely overwhelming the enemy. Had he thrown forward just one more brigade, it could have driven Doubleday off of McPherson Ridge and back into the town.

Heth's immediate superior, Lt. Gen. A. P. Hill, was nearly five miles away at the Cashtown Inn. As was becoming the norm, he was sick and lying on a cot. Meanwhile, Lee and his second in command, Lt. Gen. James Longstreet, were still making their way to Cashtown along a road that had bottlenecked because of the fighting.

Despite the lack of leadership, Heth still nearly blundered to victory. Buford, Reynolds, and Doubleday had to work miracles to hold him out of Gettysburg. Now, as Federal reinforcements continued to arrive on the field, Doubleday's men consolidated their position, and Heth's opportunity slipped away.

That didn't mean the Confederates were through.

At the Railroad Cut

Although the railroad had come *to* Gettysburg in the 1850s, it had not made its way *through* Gettysburg. The Pennsylvania Rail Road line from Hanover terminated at the western edge of the town at North Washington Street. A western rail bed had been excavated, but the tracks had yet to be laid.

The railroad bed on the western side of town had three distinct "cuts." The first cut was a few hundred yards northwest of the Reynolds/Buford monuments. The second cut, or middle cut, bisects the modern park road, which crosses the cut via a bridge. The third cut was roughly perpendicular to the Seminary. All three of the cuts were deep—as evidenced even to this day—thus fighting from them was tough.

The Federals who fought in this area were under the able division command of Brig. Gen. James Wadsworth. Prior to the war, Wadsworth had studied law at Harvard and dabbled in politics. During the First Manassas campaign, he proved a capable staff officer to Brig. Gen. Irvin McDowell. The following month, in August of 1861, Wadsworth was promoted to brigadier general and held the post of military governor of Washington, D.C. In 1862, while serving in the army, he ran for New York's governorship but lost. The following year, at Chancellorsville, he commanded the I Corps' 1st Division. Wadsworth was mortally wounded at the battle of the Wilderness in 1864 and died a few days later. A monument there marks the spot.

The 55th North Carolina, entering their first battle, lost their colonel, John Connally, who was described by fellow Confederate officer Dorsey Pender as "a most conceited fellow." In the spring of 1863, when Connally was insulted by a report written by an Alabama officer, he and Alfred Belo challenged the offending officer to a duel with Mississippi rifles at 40 paces. Both sides were poor

In 1859, Gettysburg's fine new rail station was dedicated along Carlisle Street. (dw)

As a soldier, the 55-year-old James Wadsworth defied convention. He wasn't a West Point graduate, nor was he a career politician like many other generals; he was a millionaire New Yorker from Geneseo who had answered his country's call to arms and had even refused pay for his service. (loc)

shots and, in the end, the Alabama officer apologized for the slight against Connally's regiment.

Due to the two wounds Connally suffered on July 1, he was left behind as the army retreated to Virginia. Federal surgeons, who took custody of him, had to amputate his left arm. Connally was paroled in March of 1864 but was unable to take to the field again. In the postwar years, he moved to Texas and then to Virginia, where he served in the state legislature, becoming the youngest man elected to the state senate. On April 27, 1870, the third floor of the Virginia state house collapsed into the Hall of the House of Delegates below. In the "great disaster," 61 people were killed and 251 injured, but amazingly Connally survived. He lived to the age of 64.

Connally's second in command, Alfred Belo almost became a Federal captive, too. While trying to make his way out of the railroad cut and back to Herr's Ridge, a Federal swung a sword at his head, nearly hitting him. He and a number of the 55th were able to scramble to safety.

Rufus Dawes, the epitome of a citizen-soldier, was the great grandson of Revolutionary War hero William Dawes, the man who made the midnight ride with Paul Revere. Rufus was also the father of Charles Dawes, vice president of the United States during the Coolidge Administration. The Marietta College alum was an Ohio native, even though he commanded the 6th Wisconsin.

After Frank Waller captured the flag of the 2nd Mississippi, Dawes trumped his corporal. The Federals sealed off the second cut with artillery, and then Dawes' adjutant swung a detachment of 20 men into the cut. "[W]e were immediately upon the enemy, with a general cry from our men of: 'Throw down your muskets. Down with your muskets,'" Dawes wrote.

> *Running quickly forward through the line of men, I found myself face to face with at least a thousand rebels, who I looked down upon in the railroad cut, which was here about four feet deep. Adjutant Brooks, equal to the emergency, had quickly placed men across the cut in position to fire through it. . . . I shouted: "Where is the colonel of the regiment?" An officer in gray, with stars on his collar, who stood among the men in the cut, said: "Who are you?" I said: "I am commander of this regiment. Surrender, or I will fire on you." The officer replied not a word, but promptly handed me his sword, and all his men, who still held them, threw down their muskets. . . .*

Dawes captured seven officers and 225 enlisted men from Davis' brigade, including Maj. John Blair of the 2nd Mississippi, who turned his sword over to Dawes.

The assault on the railroad cut had been costly for

A monument to the
6th Wisconsin now stands
along the railroad cut
(left-most monument).
It was purchased at the cost
of $500 and dedicated
on June 30, 1888. (loc)

the 6th Wisconsin, though. The Badgers lost 165 men in their short fight. Most of the casualties came during the advance from the Chambersburg Pike to the cut. Dawes recalled one of his soldiers that fell in the charge. "Our bravest and best are cold in the ground or suffering on beds of anguish," he wrote. "One young man, Corporal James Kelley of Company B, shot through the breast came staggering up to me before he fell and, opening his shirt, to show the wound said, Colonel, won't you write to my folks that I died a soldier?"

Among the Confederates who fell into Dawes' hands was Cpl. William Murphy, the color-bearer who had lost his flag earlier in the fight. Murphy was taken to Fort Delaware, a Federal fort/prison in the middle of the Delaware River. Within weeks, he escaped and made his way back to the army. He was given leave home and captured by the 5th Ohio Cavalry at Corinth, Mississippi. Murphy was taken back to Fort Delaware and paroled on June 13, 1865. In later life, Murphy corresponded with Dawes, asking that his flag be returned so that he could "see it once more in my life. . . ." The flag was returned to the state of Mississippi on 1905.

➡ TO STOP 7

Continue on Reynolds Avenue North. Ahead, you will see a stop sign at the intersection of Reynolds Avenue North, Buford Avenue, and Wadsworth Avenue. Turn left onto Buford Avenue and proceed to the stop sign at the intersection with the Mummasburg Road. Proceed through the stop sign onto Confederate Avenue. You will notice that the Eternal Peace Light Memorial dominates the landscape. There is ample parking; get out of your vehicle and walk up to the memorial.

GPS: 39 50.894 N, 77 14.599 W

CHAPTER SEVEN

JULY 1 1863

In an army full of eccentrics, Lt. Gen. Richard S. Ewell, commander of Lee's Second Corps, stood out as perhaps the quirkiest of all.

Ewell was one of Lee's most respected officers heading into the Gettysburg campaign—enough so that Lee had tapped him to take the place of the fallen Thomas Jonathan "Stonewall" Jackson. Ewell had worked well under Jackson and held the respect of the men of Second Corps, as well as the men on Jackson's old staff, whom Ewell retained.

That sat well with Alexander "Sandie" Pendleton, Jackson's former chief of staff, who went on to serve in that same capacity for Ewell. "The more I see of him the more I am pleased to be with him," Pendleton admitted. "In some traits of character he is very much like General Jackson, especially in total disregard of his own comfort and safety. . . . He is so thoroughly honest, too, and has only one desire, to conquer The Yankees. I look for great things of him, and am glad to say that our troops have for him a good deal of the same feeling they had towards General [Stonewall] Jackson."

In many ways, though, the highly profane general was the antithesis of the pious Jackson and the courtly Lee.

Artillerist E. Porter Alexander described Ewell's "bald head, & bright eyes, & his long nose (like a wood cock's . . .)," which earned Ewell the nickname "Old Bald-Head"—"Old Baldy" for short. He was, said one observer,

a compound of anomalies, the oddest, most eccentric genius in the Confederate Army. . . . No man had a better heart nor a worse manner of showing it. He was in truth as tender and sympathetic as a woman, but, even under the slight provocation, he became externally

War and peace stand together on Oak Hill. (cm)

*as rough as a polar bear, and the needles with which
he pricked sensibilities were more numerous and keener
than porcupine quills. His written orders were full,
accurate, and lucid; but his verbal orders or directions,
especially when under intense excitement, no man could
comprehend. At such times his eyes would flash with a
peculiar brilliancy, and his brain far outran his tongue.*

A Virginia native and a graduate of the West Point
class of 1840, Ewell had put together a solid fighting
record early in the war until wounded in the left knee at
Brawner's farm during the battle of Groveton. Ewell's left
leg was amputated, and Ewell was slow to recover from the
wound. Ewell sat on the sidelines for a total of nine months
before returning to active duty. During his convalescence,
he married his first cousin, Lizinka Campbell Brown, a
childhood sweetheart who'd since become widowed. After
their marriage, Ewell still absentmindedly referred to her
as "my wife, Mrs. Brown."

Due to his wound, Ewell had taken to riding in a
carriage, but he could take to horse if necessary, and "not
only rode in battle like a cow-boy on the plains," said
one observer, "but in the whirlwind of the strife his brain
acted with the precision and rapidity of a Gatling gun."

On July 1, 1863, at around noon, as though conjuring
the spirit of his fallen former commander, Richard
Stoddert Ewell suddenly appeared on the Federal army's
unsuspecting right flank.

*   *   *

Ewell and his 21,806-man Second Corps had
performed outstanding work in the campaign thus far.
Moving down the Shenandoah Valley, they had won
stunning victories at Second Winchester (June 13-15) and
Stephenson's Depot (June 14), capturing 3,856 men, 23
cannon, more than 200,000 rounds of ammunition, 300
supply wagons, and more than 300 horses.

Moving into south-central Pennsylvania, they
foraged valuable supplies, then moved northward
and nearly captured the state capital, Harrisburg.
Only a message from Lee kept Ewell from making the
attempt: the commanding general was concentrating
the army and needed the Second Corps "to proceed
to Cashtown or Gettysburg, as circumstances might
dictate." By the evening of June 30, two-thirds of the
corps was just more than 10 miles north of Gettysburg
in the area of Heidlersberg.

On the morning of July 1, Ewell decided that the
Second Corps would make for Cashtown. But as the
march started, Ewell received another message from

Hill, stating "he was advancing upon Gettysburg. . . ." Ewell quickly changed the Second Corps' course: he sent one of his divisions down the Old Harrisburg Road towards Gettysburg; a second division was to proceed down the Carlisle Road. That would bring butternut soldiers down on Gettysburg from the north and northeast. Ewell's final division, laden with the spoils reaped from the Pennsylvania countryside, would cut southwest towards the Chambersburg Pike.

Oak Hills offers a panoramic view down McPherson's Ridge. (cm)

To inform Lee of the new marching orders, Ewell dispatched his adjutant, Maj. Campbell Brown—his stepson—to find the commanding general. Brown found Lee somewhere between Cashtown and Gettysburg along the Chambersburg Pike. Once Brown informed Lee of the new marching orders, Lee responded by asking if either the staff officer or General Ewell knew the whereabouts of Jeb Stuart. The chief of Lee's cavalry, it seemed, was missing.

Brown told Lee that they had no knowledge of the cavalry chief's location. Lee then stressed "'very strongly,' that a general engagement was to be avoided until the arrival of the rest of the army."

Like it or not, though, the general engagement Lee wanted to avoid was already erupting just a few miles to the east, courtesy of Harry Heth—and Ewell was walking right into it.

*   *   *

A mile to the north of McPherson's farm, Oak Hill loomed over the fields where, shortly before, Lysander Cutler's men had grappled with Joseph Davis'. As both sides tried to catch their breath, Federals also consolidated their position and Confederates sent more artillery to the front—33 guns in all. Confederates started hammering the Federal line anew.

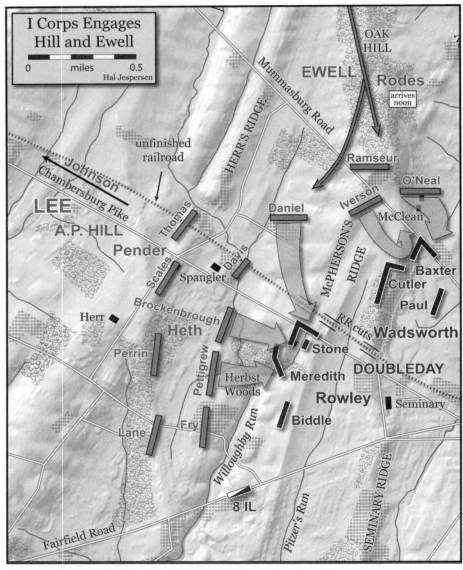

I CORPS ENGAGES HILL AND EWELL—In the morning, the Federal I Corps rushed reinforcements onto the field in just enough strength to fend off assaults from the Confederate Third Corps. Even as a lull in the action allowed both sides to catch their breath, elements of the Confederate Second Corps appeared on the north end of the field. Confederates attacked on both fronts.

On Oak Hill, Richard Ewell materialized from the treeline. With him was his juniormost division commander, Maj. Gen. Robert Rodes. Together, they watched the renewed fighting, realizing they were perfectly positioned to fall on the Federal flank.

Rodes was entering his second full battle as a

division commander, and unlike his boss, he looked every inch the soldier—one of "the most splendid looking officers of the war," one soldier said. An 1848 graduate of the Virginia Military Institute, Rodes later returned to his alma mater to teach. He then made his way to the Deep South to work as a civil engineer on numerous railroad projects from Texas to Alabama, finally settling in the latter state. Just before the outbreak of war, Rodes accepted an offer to return to VMI to again teach, but when hostilities erupted, he instead assumed command of the 5th Alabama Infantry. The Virginian was a stern disciplinarian, but his officers and men respected him; he also earned the admiration of superiors likes of Daniel Harvey Hill, Ewell, and Jackson. "I like him so much," said Second Corps staff officer James Power Smith. "He is very much admired by all and very popular."

Historian Douglas Southall Freeman described Maj. Gen. Robert Rodes as a "Norse God." (loc)

By the Gettysburg campaign, Rodes had quietly put together one of the most solid fighting records in the Army of Northern Virginia. At brigade command, he had performed admirably on the Peninsula, as well as at South Mountain, Antietam, and Fredericksburg. At Chancellorsville, Rodes was temporary division commander of D. H. Hill's division, with his division in the lead for Jackson's audacious flank attack. Following Jackson's wounding during the battle, and then the subsequent wounding of A. P. Hill, Rodes served as the temporary commander of the Second Corps, although he quickly turned command over to the more experienced Jeb Stuart.

The day after the close of the Chancellorsville campaign, Lee forwarded Rodes' name for promotion to President Jefferson Davis. "I desire Genl Rodes to command D.H. Hill's old Division," Lee stated. "He is a good soldier who behaved admirably in the last battle and deserves promotion." Rodes would turn out to be the only non-West Point graduate to command a division in Lee's army at Gettysburg.

Rodes had been ill as he approached Gettysburg, but as soon as he and Ewell assessed the situation, he set to work deploying his infantry atop Oak Hill. To bolster the line, Rodes deployed Lt. Col. Thomas H. Carter's eight artillery pieces, targeting McPherson's Woods and the area around the railroad cut. That enabled Confederates to enfilade the entire I Corps line.

Because most of their attention was focused due south, Ewell and Rodes did not at first see the newly arriving Federal troops on an open plain to the southeast of Oak Hill. These were soldiers of Oliver Otis Howard's XI Corps, streaming onto the battlefield from the north edge of town. Rodes did finally notice them, though, and he responded by placing artillery on the eastern slope of

Oak Ridge dominated the Gettysburg plain, which stretched out to the east. (loc)

Oak Hill, which dominated the plain below. Soon, his guns were all "warmly engaged."

In possession of the strong position at Oak Hill, and with his and Hill's batteries all playing on the enemy, Ewell decided to press the enemy. "It was too late to avoid an engagement without abandoning the position already taken up," he later explained, "and I determined to push the attack vigorously."

Like his predecessor, Ewell found the enemy's flank and was prepared to exploit his advantage. It looked as though Lee truly had found his second Stonewall Jackson.

At Oak Hill

The Army of Northern Virginia seemed to have the knack of locating the best artillery position on a battlefield. Be it by design or by luck, Rebel gunners often held the best real estate, if not the best guns on the field. At Antietam, they held Nicodemius Heights; at Fredericksburg, it was Marye's Heights; at Chancellorsville, it was Hazel Grove. Here on the first day at Gettysburg, it was Oak Hill.

Oak Hill gave the Confederates a beautiful panorama of the field. To the south, they could see all the way down the I Corps line to where the ground slopes down toward the Fairfield Road. They could also see Little and Big Round Top in the distance. To the east, they could see all the way to Rock Creek, near the modern radio tower, as well as to the York Road (visitors might be able to spy the Hampton Inn along Route 30 East). To the southeast, they could see the town, Cemetery Hill and, farther away, Benner's Hill.

This portion of Oak Hill was located on the 112-acre John S. Forney farm. Forney and his wife, Mary, had purchased the farm in 1862. Their home once stood behind the 17th Pennsylvania Cavalry monument at the intersection of Mummasburg Road and Buford Ave. During the battle, the Forneys, with their six-month-old daughter, retreated to the home of Mary's father, who lived along Baltimore Street. When they Forneys returned home after the fight, they found that "everything about the place was completely destroyed by the battle except the house and barn, and they were well riddled by shot and shell." The home survived until the 1930s when it was destroyed to make way for the new Peace Light Memorial.

The Peace Light Memorial is the largest monument on the first-day battlefield (see Appendix H). Of the nearly 1,400 monuments and markers on the battlefield at Gettysburg, the Peace Light Memorial is the only monument with the word "Peace" in its name.

From the area around the Peace Light Memorial, Rodes' division set off a series of attacks on the Federal line. Numerically, it was the largest division on field at Gettysburg. The rolls of June 30, 1863, showed 8,474 officers and men, although in reality only about 7,900 of Rodes' men participated in the battle. Rodes and three of his brigade commanders—Junius Daniel, George Doles, and Stephen Ramseur—all would perish within five months of one another in 1864.

Behind the Peace Light Memorial are two special cannon known as Whitworth Guns. These guns made up a section of Hurt's Alabama Battery on Oak Hill. The 2.75-inch guns are unique in that they were breech-loading—cannon loaded from the rear rather than the front. The guns were also made of steel, while the other guns on the field were made of either iron or bronze.

The British-made Whitworths had the ability to fire a round nearly six full miles, making them the longest-ranged cannon on the field at Gettysburg. (dw)

→ **TO STOP 8**

Continue straight on Confederate Avenue to the stop sign at its intersection of the Mummasburg Road. Proceed straight through the stop sign onto Doubleday Avenue. Ahead on the left is an Observation Tower; pull over and park on the left.

GPS: 39 84.406 N, 77 24.189 W

Oak Ridge

CHAPTER EIGHT
JULY 1 1863

With Stonewall Jackson's heir apparent overseeing the operation, and with one of the most capable division commanders in the entire Army of Northern Virginia executing it, the Confederate assault from Oak Hill had all the makings of another crushing Chancellorsvillesque flank attack.

But it bungled almost from the first steps.

Rodes personally oversaw the deployment of his troops, choosing two brigades for the main attack. Four North Carolina regiments under Brig. Gen. Alfred Iverson would advance from the Forney homestead area, while Rodes' old brigade, now under Col. Edward O'Neal, would attack with four of its five Alabama regiments.

A third brigade, consisting of five North Carolina regiments under Brig. Gen. Junius Daniel, would support Iverson "if necessary;" if not necessary, then Daniel was "to attack on his [Iverson's] right as soon as possible."

Rodes aimed for the right flank of the I Corps, with aspirations of rolling down the Federal battle line and sweeping the enemy from the field.

With the Federal XI Corps arriving north of town, though, Rodes decided to protect his position by leaving his fourth brigade—the four regiments of Brig. Gen. George Doles—on the plain along the Carlisle Road. When Ewell's second division arrived on the field, Doles would act as the link between the two Second Corps divisions.

It was 2:00 p.m.: time for Rodes' subordinates to carry forward the assault—and here's where the bungling began.

O'Neal's men stepped off early. Making matters worse, O'Neal did not advance with them. He remained behind and, someone noted, "he and his staff officers were not mounted, and he had no mounted men with

The "Stalwart Oak Tree," dedicated on September 3, 1888, honors the 90th Pennsylvania Infantry, which served on Oak Ridge on the afternoon of July 1. (cm)

him"—which meant that if orders were required to go to the front, they would not arrive in a timely manner.

Inexplicably, Iverson didn't advance with his men, either.

An unseen trap awaited them all.

*   *   *

The stone wall Baxter's men used for cover still runs along part of Oak Ridge. (cm)

Even as the morning fight at the railroad cut had ended, more Federal reinforcements came onto the field: the I Corps division of Brig. Gen. John Robinson. Doubleday split Robinson's division in two, deploying part of it along Seminary Ridge to prepare a fallback position with breastworks and deploying the other to the right end of the I Corps line at Oak Ridge.

Brigadier General Henry Baxter led the brigade that went to the ridge—six regiments in all—and halted his men near the Mummasburg Road. Rodes' arrival on Oak Hill thwarted Doubleday's defense, so the Federal commander improvised by ending the line at Oak Ridge and turning the line back toward the Gettysburg plain. The XI Corps could then tie in there.

Understanding the precariousness of his position, Baxter deployed skirmishers to the north of the Mummasburg Road, then hunkered the rest of his men behind a stone wall for cover, their flags furled so as not to give away their position. And then they waited.

Rodes wanted to make a three-brigade assault, which, in theory, would have swept Baxter's men from Oak Ridge and flushed Cutler's men from an adjacent woodlot. But it was not to be.

Instead of advancing four regiments of Alabamians as Rodes had intended, O'Neal sent forward only three, fronted by what one soldier called "a cloud of busy skirmishers." Later, O'Neal claimed that he was deprived of two regiments personally assigned by Rodes to link with Doles on the left and Daniel on the right. Instead of clarifying the roles of these regiments in the assault, O'Neal pouted and sent the rest of his men to their demise. Elements of four Federal regiments poured fire into them.

"With the sharp crack of the muskets a fleecy cloud of smoke rolled down the front of the brigade," one Federal said, "and the Minie balls zipped and buzzed with a merry chorus toward the Southern line." The Alabamians never reached the Federal line, thrown back in great confusion well before they even reached the Mummasburg Road.

O'Neal's inaccurate and disingenuous report of the battle claimed that "[w]e were compelled to fall back as the regiment on the extreme left, being flanked by a superior force of the enemy, gave way. It was impossible to hold the position we had gained, as the enemy had the advantage in numbers and position." He looked to lay the blame at the feet of the 5th Alabama—Rodes' former command—who, at the time, were engaging in a brisk skirmish with arriving XI Corps troops.

Rodes, already disgusted by O'Neal's poor performance at Chancellorsville, would find the Gettysburg debacle too much to tolerate. Lee would agree, withholding from O'Neal a brigadier general's commission, dated from June 6, 1863. By the middle of July, O'Neal was ousted from brigade command, and by early 1864 he was shipped out of the Army of Northern Virginia for good.

Iverson, too, seemed determine to continue the streak of bad luck plaguing the Army of Northern Virginia at the brigade level. Iverson was a Georgia native leading four North Carolina regiments to battle. His men were veteran fighters who outwardly loathed their brigade commander.

Iverson was the son of a well-to-do senator who obtained a commission for his 17-year-old son during the Mexican-American War. After the war, Iverson stayed with the military and served until the outbreak of the Civil War. His father intervened again, obtaining for him colonel's stars and command of the 20th North Carolina. Iverson served admirably through the 1862 campaigns. In November 1862, he was given brigade command, but his tenure was marked by intense controversy with his subordinates.

Now at Gettysburg, Iverson was near the Forney farm house when he sent his brigade forward into action. "Give them hell," he said—and watched them go.

Hell was waiting for them.

*   *   *

Because the O'Neal's and Iverson's attacks were disjointed, Henry Baxter's Federal brigade was able to meet the Confederate threat in two distinct actions.

During O'Neal's assault, the bulk of Baxter's brigade had faced north/north-east along the Mummasburg road. Now division commander Robinson refaced the Federal line, ordering the brigade to change front. Thus, the battle line shifted from its alignment on the Mummasburg Road to an alignment along the stone

Edward O'Neal's poor performance at Chancellorsville had already earned him the ire of his commanding officer, Robert Rodes. His performance on July 1 proved to be the nail in his coffin. (loc)

At Chancellorsville, Alfred Iverson's men had fought well, although some attempted to accuse the Georgian of cowardice. (loc)

The 2,995 Federals on Oak Ridge were commanded by Brig. Gen. John C. Robinson. In an age of wildly bearded men, Robinson was reportedly the hairiest man in the Army of the Potomac. His monument (below) stands today at the intersection of Doubleday and Robinson Avenues behind the small observation tower. (loc; cm)

wall facing west toward the Forney farm buildings. "Behind the stone wall, the Union soldiers, with rifles cocked and fingers in the triggers, waited and bided their time, feeling confident that they could throw back these regiments coming against them," a member of the 88th Pennsylvania remembered.

With no skirmishers in front, no support on the flanks, and an inactive brigade commander somewhere off in the rear, the oncoming Tar Heels seemed ripe for disaster. "[They] reached and ascended a little gully or depression in the ground and, moving on, ascended the opposite slope as if on brigade drill," said a Federal who watched the North Carolinians advance. They were fully unaware of what awaited them, said a member of the 12th North Carolina, "not knowing certainly where the enemy was, for his whole line, with every flag, was concealed behind the rock wall on their right and the drop in the ground on their left. Not one of them was to be seen."

Suddenly from their front came a solid sheet of flame and smoke. Nearly 1,500 muskets discharged at once. Unsuspecting officers and men fell by the scores. "[R]arely has such a destructive volley been fired on any field of battle," said a survivor.

Load and fire! Load and fire! was the order up and down the Federal line. "A steady death-dealing fire was kept up," wrote Samuel Boone of the 88th Pennsylvania, "our men loading in comparative safety, and then resting rifle on shoulders before them, would fire coolly and with unerring aim."

Iverson's men attempted to press on. "We advanced to a gully about eighty yards in front of the rock wall," Lt. Joseph B. Oliver of the 20th North Carolina later wrote. "Here we halted, for by this time our ranks were so depleted it was impossible to carry the strong position in front."

After a few minutes, it became clear that the North Carolinians had stalled. Colonel Charles Wheelock of the 97th New York advanced. "A sally was made by part of the brigade . . ." wrote Col. Richard Coulter of the 11th Pennsylvania, "which resulted in the capture of about 500 of the enemy."

Survivors surrendered when allowed, which later lead to wholly unwarranted allegations of cowardice. Rodes attempted to remedy these allegations in his report: "Iverson's left being thus exposed, heavy loss was inflicted upon his brigade. His men fought and died like heroes. His dead lay in a distinctly marked line of battle."

John Robinson summed it up more succinctly: the enemy was "handsomely repulsed. . . ."

Many of Iverson's wounded were taken back to the

Forney home, including the colonel of the 23rd North Carolina, Daniel H. Christie, who was mortally wounded in the assault. As he was taken to the rear, Christie was overcome by the reality that he would not live to lead his men back into action, ". . . but he would see that 'The Imbecile Iverson never should.'" Robert E. Lee and Robert Rodes saw to this. Iverson was transferred to the Western Theater, never to fight in the Army of Northern Virginia again.

Such had been the story for the Army of Northern Virginia all day: failures at the brigade level made it impossible for Confederates to get any real traction in the battle. Archer had fought well but had been roughly handled by superior numbers and a superior foe. Davis' men at the railroad cut had started off even better, but lacking a brigade commander at the front and losing regimental commanders and unit cohesion during the battle cost them. O'Neal failed at Oak Ridge, then Iverson, too.

Rodes fared no better in his attempts to dislodge the I Corps from the north than Heth had off to the west.

Ewell was far from through, though. Once more, he prepared to turn the tactical situation on its side.

At Oak Ridge

It may seem the Oak Ridge area has a disproportionate number of monuments. This is due to the fact that an entire Federal division was shuffled in and out of this area over the early afternoon of July 1.

The observation tower on Oak Ridge gives visitors a great perspective of the area north of Gettysburg. The tower is one of five wooden towers originally built on the Gettysburg battlefield, later replaced by three metal structures, including this one. The other two stand along West Confederate Ave. and atop Culp's Hill.

Near the intersection of Doubleday Avenue and the Mummasburg Road stands one of the battlefield's most distinctive monuments, the "Stalwart Oak Tree." The monument tells the story of an incident that allegedly happened to the unit: an artillery shell crashed into a tree somewhere atop the hill, and a robin's nest fell to the ground. One of the members of the regiment climbed the tree

Lined up along Oak Ridge: monuments to the 12th Massachusetts, the 88th Pennsylvania, the 83rd New York, the 97th New York, the 11th Pennsylvania, the 107th Pennsylvania, the 16th Maine, and the 94th New York. (cm)

and replaced the nest—which can now be seen near the top of the monument, along with the artillery shell and various accouterments from the soldiers.

Another, less conspicuous monument stands within yards of the Stalwart Oak. Dedicated October 3, 1889, the monument marks the bravery of the 16th Maine Infantry. The unit's 298 men were ordered to be the rear guard for the sector as the I Corps troops poured back toward Gettysburg, driven into retreat by Ewell's corps late on July 1. By the end of the battle, the 16th Maine had lost 232 men. Their battle flag became imperiled in the fighting withdrawal, so the surviving men ripped their flag from the staff and cut it into small pieces, giving each member a piece of the flag so that their beloved colors would not fall into the hands of the foe.

In front of the stone wall held by Robinson's division are the fields from where Iverson's men advanced. Once they pinned the Tar Heels down, men of the 97th New York, 11th Pennsylvania, and 88th Pennsylvania went out from the works to capture the tempting Southern battle flags in their front.

Cannonball, bird, knapsack, rifle, vine—all combine to turn the "Stalwart Oak" into a story as well as a memorial. (cm)

The flagstaff of the 20th North Carolina was ripped from the hands of Lt. John D. Irvin and later presented to Col. Charles Wheelock of the 97th New York. Wheelock took his sword and attempted to take the flag from the staff, but in doing so he cut the flag in two. As Federals were later driven from this position, a member of the 45th North Carolina was able to recapture half of the 20th's battle flag. Fifty years after the battle, members of the 97th New York and 20th North Carolina came together at Gettysburg for the anniversary of the battle. During the event, Sgt. Henry Fitzgerald of the 97th New York sought out any members of the 20th. He was finally presented to John Irvin, "the very man we took it [the flag] from," Fitzgerald recounted. He presented Irvin with the other half of the 20th's flag.

The flag of the 23rd North Carolina also fell into Federal hands along Oak Ridge. A small monument about 30 yards in front of the large 88th Pennsylvania monument along Doubleday Avenue marks the approximate location. Sergeant Edward L. Gilligan used the butt of his rifle to relieve the 23rd's color-bearer of his flag. Gilligan survived the battle and Civil War. For his actions on July 1, he was awarded the Medal of Honor.

In the field near the 88th Pennsylvania's smaller monument is the area of where Iverson's assault came aground. In these fields, one Confederate later saw, by actual count, 79 corpses in a straight line, "perfectly dressed." Three of the men had fallen forward; the remaining 76 had fallen upon their backs. Many of the men were later interred in large burial trenches, now

The 16th Maine has two monuments within a couple hundred feet of each other. The tall obelisk, dedicated in 1889, marks their position during the afternoon's fighting (left). (cm)

famously called "Iverson's Pits." The historian of the 12th North Carolina described them:

In the lowest part of the depression, in the rear if the battleground of Iverson's brigade, four hallow pits were dug by prisoners, in which were buried the dead of that brigade. The surface of these pits is to be easily distinguished . . . from the surrounding ground on account of the more luxuriant growth of grass and crops over them.

As the I Corps was forced to fall back to a more consolidated position along Seminary Ridge, the 16th Maine took up position as the rear guard. They engaged in a fighting retreat all the way back to the railroad cut, where the regiment was finally overwhelmed. Out of 275 men engaged, 11 were killed, 62 were wounded, and 159 were taken prisoner, most of them at the railroad cut. A small monument marks the location where their stalwart defense began (above). (cm)

The death and destruction among the 5th, 20th, and 23rd North Carolina regiments was appalling. The 23rd lost 23 officers and 264 enlisted men out of 316 engaged. The 5th North Carolina lost 289 out of 473 engaged, and the 20th North Carolina—Iverson's old regiment—lost 253 out of 372 engaged. Only the 12th North Carolina was spared from such disaster; the small ridgeline 150 yards in front of the Federal line shielded them. The 12th lost only 79 men out of 219 engaged.

Finally, along Doubleday Avenue stands a monument topped by a soldier prepared to face the enemy. The back side of the monument faces the road, but on the front of the monument is a small sculpture of a dog. Her name was Sallie, the mascot of the 11th Pennsylvania Infantry. Sallie was said to hate only three things in life: "Rebels, Democrats, and Women." She was the pride and joy of the regiment, though. She knew drum calls, stood at dress parade, and stayed beside her comrades in battle.

On July 1, Sallie's regiment was pushed off the field, and Sallie became separated from them. The little dog made her way to the old battle line, where she remained among the fallen of the regiment. After the battle, another unit in Baxter's brigade found Sallie and returned her to her regiment. Sallie fought alongside her brothers in arms

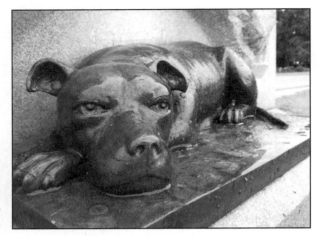

Sallie the War Dog (right) remains faithful to the men of the 11th Pennsylvania, still curled at the feet of the bronze sentry who stands atop their monument (opposite). (cm)

at Spotsylvania Court House, where in 1864, she was wounded in the neck. Still the little dog stayed in the army, remaining until February 6, 1865, when she was killed in action at the battle of Hatcher's Run.

→ **TO STOP 9**

Continue on Doubleday Avenue and make a left on Robinson Avenue. You will proceed down the backside of Oak Ridge to the intersection of Robinson Avenue and the Mummasburg Road. At the stop sign, turn right and proceed 0.3 miles. Ahead on the left is Howard Avenue. Turn left onto Howard Avenue. The first monument and set of cannons ahead on the right commemorates Hubert Dilger's Battery I, 1st Ohio Light. Parking may be limited.

GPS: 39 50.515 N, 77 14.033 W

The XI Corps Arrives

CHAPTER NINE
JULY 1 1863

In the days following the battle of Chancellorsville, Capt. Fred Winkler had a bad case of the blues. Winkler, of the 26th Wisconsin, had been among the XI Corps men routed at that battle by Stonewall Jackson's surprise flank attack. His after-battle assessment summed up the attitudes of his bedraggled comrades. "[V]ery little confidence is felt in General Howard," he said. "Troops without confidence in their leaders are worth nothing."

These were the troops, and this was the general, who appeared next on the Gettysburg battlefield to reinforce Doubleday's beleaguered line.

At around 1:00 p.m., as A. P. Hill renewed the artillery barrage from the west and as Richard Ewell and Robert Rodes began to organize their assault from Oak Hill, the lead elements of the Federal XI Corps began to stream out of the northern edge of Gettysburg. They formed at a right angle to the I Corps line at the top of Oak Ridge, thus "refusing" the line so that Confederates could not flank their position. Unfortunately, their line mostly ran across a wide plain with little cover.

With 9,242 men, the Union XI corps was the smallest infantry corps to fight at the battle. About 60 percent of the men and officers were of German descent. Prior to the Chancellorsville campaign, their much-beloved commander, Maj. Gen. Franz Sigel, was replaced with Howard. The men, who used to rally behind the cry "I fights mit Sigel," were none too happy with the switch.

Howard was a Maine native, an alumnus of Bowdoin College, and an 1854 graduate of West Point, where he was fourth in his class. At the outbreak of the war, Howard accepted the colonelcy of the 3rd Maine Infantry, and he rose to brigade commander at Bull Run. At the battle of Seven Pines, he was wounded in the right

"Old Leatherbritches" commanded the Federal artillery that leap-frogged out to this advanced position. (cm)

James, Henry, and Edward Fahnestock owned a dry goods store on Baltimore Street (right). After the battle, the United States Sanitary Commission used the building as its base of operations as it assisted with the aftermath of battle. The building still stands (below). (achs; cm)

arm, which was subsequently amputated. His actions there, though, earned him the Medal of Honor.

When Howard returned to the army, he was given a division in the II Corps, where, during the December 1862 river crossing at Fredericksburg, his men performed well—no thanks to their commander, who seemed to lead from too far in the rear. Yet on the eve of the Chancellorsville campaign, the 32-year-old Howard had been given command of the XI Corps.

"Howard . . . is brave enough and a most perfect gentleman," a fellow officer said of him. "He is a Christian as well as a man of ability, but there is some doubt as to his having snap enough to manage the Germans who require to be ruled with an iron rod." Howard treated the men well, though, and because of that, they generally liked him despite his stern demeanor. They gave him the nickname of "Old Prayer Book," although others gave him the unflattering nickname of "Uh Oh" Howard—a name that would, unfortunately, become all-too-appropriate.

At Chancellorsville, Howard's XI Corps was embarrassingly swept from the field by Stonewall Jackson's surprise flank attack on May 2. The corps was thus labeled with the unflattering nicknames of "The Flying Crescent," after their crescent-shaped corps symbol, or the "Flying Dutchmen," a dig at their German heritage. "I wanted to die," the humiliated Howard later said.

Howard arrived in Gettysburg near 10:00 a.m. on July 1. He first rode over to Cemetery Hill and inspected the topography there, then made his way into the town—and inexplicably decided not to ride forward and meet his commanding officer, John Reynolds. Instead, Howard, under his own volition, made his way down Baltimore Street on a reconnaissance mission.

Howard looked for "some method of getting into the belfry of the courthouse," he later explained, "when my attention was called . . . to the Fahnestock

observatory across the street." Howard made for the rooftop. "Mounting to the top, I was delighted with the opened view," penned Howard. "With maps and field glasses we examined the battlefield."

Howard's view of the battlefield revealed the inherent indefensibility of the wide plain—more than a mile of open farmland that offered virtually no military advantages. The XI Corps had to deploy there, though, to protect the I Corps' flank. With his burn at Chancellorsville fresh in his mind, he ordered his men into position, paying special mind to protect his flanks. He also held back one of his divisions as a reserve, posting them on a hilltop south of town. The high ground there—Cemetery Hill—offered an ideal fallback position should things on the front go awry. It was, all in all, a "safe" decision.

Shortly thereafter, Howard received word of Reynolds's death. By virtue of seniority, Howard rose to take Reynolds' place as commander of the army's Left Wing.

Howard dictated orders to Doubleday, telling him to retain command of I Corps; he sent word to Buford, telling him to retain command of his forces; and finally he sent word to XI Corps division commander Maj. Gen. Carl Schurz to assume command of the corps. Buford, ironically, would later say, "[T]here seems to be no directing person," although Howard himself sent him orders.

The field was now in Howard's hands—a field that he would not personally visit for nearly three full hours.

ABOVE: Historian Frank O'Reilly has called the one-armed Maj. Gen. Oliver Otis Howard "pious but vapid." (loc)

TOP: As an old man, Howard revisited the battlefield and once more ascended to the roof of the Fahnestock building. (*)

*   *   *

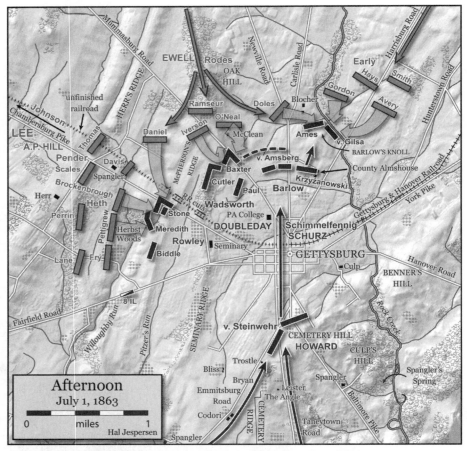

AFTERNOON—After a tough morning of battle along McPherson Ridge, the Federal I Corps got a reprieve as Confederates regrouped. During the lull, the Confederate Second Corps appeared on the north end of the field atop Oak Hill. The Federals responded by hunkering down on Oak Ridge and using the newly arrived XI Corps to refuse the flank, extending the line eastward across the Gettysburg plain. When Confederates renewed the fight, they attacked from the west and north.

As Howard assumed the role of acting wing commander, his senior division commander, Maj. Gen. Carl Schurz, took on the role of acting corps commander.

Schurz was a colorful character whose life story reads like a Hollywood script. Born in Germany, the highly educated officer had taken a circuitous route to the Union ranks. A former German revolutionary on the losing side, he ping-ponged around Europe until, in 1852, he and his wife finally found themselves in America. They settled in Wisconsin, and Schurz became a staunch Republican. His political support of Lincoln earned him a commission as a brigadier general, to the chagrin of many West Point officers.

Schurz fought at Second Manassas and was up for command of the XI Corps, but Hooker had strong objections to the political appointee and appointed Howard instead. "I would consider the services of an entire corps as entirely lost to this army were it [the XI Corps] to fall into the hands of Maj. Gen. Schurz," Hooker complained.

Now serving under the man who superseded him, the 34-year-old German ordered the corps to the town on the double-quick. At around noon, the first of the XI Corps troops filed out onto the Gettysburg plain north of town and took up a line of battle.

Whether he looked more professorish than soldierly, the bespectacled Maj. Gen. Carl Schurz had an intense expression. (loc)

As the XI Corps deployed, they tried to link up with Robinson's I Corps division on Oak Ridge. While they didn't succeed—Oak Ridge's steep jump in elevation posed a challenge—four companies of the newly arrived 45th New York made their presence known. Rodes had just ordered O'Neal forward to attack Robinson on Oak Ridge; the New Yorkers appeared just in time to enfilade O'Neal's left-most regiment, the 5th Alabama, breaking their advance.

With the XI Corps' 3rd Division deployed, Schurz turned his attention across the Carlisle Road. There, he deployed the corps' 1st Division, commanded by Brig. Gen Francis C. Barlow. Within that division, he deployed one brigade between the Carlisle Road and Harrisburg Road, just behind the Adams County Alms House. He deployed the second brigade "en echelon behind the right of the First Brigade" with their right flank ending near Rock Creek.

With the stain of their collapse at Chancellorsville just two months prior still fresh in their mind, the men of the Federal XI Corps were ready for a rematch with the Confederate Second Corps.

The Adams County Almshouse stood near the Harrisburg Road. It housed debtors and the mentally ill. (NPS)

*   *   *

All of the blue troops shuffling onto the Gettysburg plain did not go unnoticed by the Confederates on Oak Hill. "General Rodes, therefore sent two batteries, and posted them on the left [of the division]," wrote Rodes' artillery commander. The Confederate cannon began battering the Gettysburg plain even as Southern infantry increased the pressure on the XI Corps' front. The 5th Alabama, recovering from the surprise fire poured into them by the New Yorkers, pulled back, and a battalion of sharpshooters took to the front. Men from George Doles' brigade, holding the left of Rodes' line, bolstered them. The Dutchmen of the XI Corps, in return, "made a strong demonstration on our left," a Confederate recalled.

To counter the Confederate artillery, Schurz brought up guns of his own. The first battery to arrive consisted

Surviving the war, Hubert Dilger stayed in the United States, and in 1884, he and his wife had a son, Anton C. Dilger. Anton was educated in Germany and had strong German ties when the First World War broke out. The young doctor came back to the Unites States in 1916 with the intention of infecting livestock with Anthrax so that the animals would be tainted and thus useless if supplied to the Allied Powers. American authorities became wise to the plan, though, and Anton fled to Mexico, then to Spain, where he died in the Spanish Flu epidemic less than one month prior to Armistice Day. While the elder Dilger was an American hero, his son was, ironically, an American traitor. (loc)

of six smoothbore Napoleon cannon commanded by a 27-year-old German native, Capt. Hubert A. C. Dilger. Dilger was a well-trained, highly motivated officer who violated army protocol by insisting on wearing a pair of lederhosen, earning him the nickname "Leatherbritches."

Dilger had been one of the first men in the Union army to detect Stonewall Jackson's famed flank attack at Chancellorsville. Unfortunately for the Yankees, no one at headquarters heeded Dilger's warning. When Jackson did come calling on the Union flank, Dilger's gunners were some of the few Federals ready for action. Dilger fought his guns along the so-called Buschbeck Line near the Wilderness Church. When he was finally forced back, he sent five of his six cannon to the rear, but he stayed behind with the last remaining gun, blasting Confederates advancing along the Orange Turnpike. Dilger would unlimber, fire, limber, and start all over. His actions earned him the Medal of Honor.

Here on the Gettysburg plain, Schurz needed the stern stuff Dilger was made of. Dilger rolled out of town and deployed into battery on a slight rise between the Mummasburg and Carlisle roads. The Confederate guns converged their fire on him. The German responded immediately. His fighting blood up, he strode over to one of his pieces, "[and] now sighted the gun himself and fired it," an artillerist recounted. "The shot dismounted a Rebel gun and killed the horses. Captain Dilger tried a second shot, sighting and firing the gun." The shot had no visible effect, so the artillerist asked, "What effect, Captain Dilger?"

Dilger, after looking through his glass, replied, "I have spiked a gun for them, plugging it at the muzzle." A private in Francis Barlow's division later confirmed the story, seeing a Rebel cannon that "had been struck in its mouth by one of our shots and flattened out."

The Confederate fire made the plain a hot position for Dilger, who requested assistance. "[A]s he had only smooth bores, he was no match for his opponent and was getting cut up badly, so I was ordered forward to help him," said Lt. William Wheeler of the 13th New York Battery. "I limbered up and went through the town at a trot, the ladies waving their handkerchiefs, and giving us all possible cheer and encouragement. I came into battery on Dilger's right, and soon showed the enemy that they had a three-inch rifled battery to contend with, and they had to shut up entirely."

Shortly after the 10 Federal guns began pounding away, Dilger's Ohioans decided to move "about five hundred yards further forward, in order to give his guns better play," an artillerist said. But as they went forward, Dilger's gunners encountered a ditch about five feet wide and four feet deep. The artillerymen went to a nearby fence and filled the ditch with the rails and took the guns across and unlimbered.

Wheeler complained that "all the shots fired too high [aimed] for [Dilger] fell into my Battery; one struck a driver of a gun and swept him and his two horses right away; strange to say, while both horses were killed, the driver only lost a leg!"

So Wheeler's men leapfrogged forward; Dilger covered.

"As we came near the place where we were to take position, we came suddenly on a very substantial fence which the men could not tear down," one of Wheeler's gunners recalled, "and we had to wait, under a very heavy fire, until axes could be brought from the caissons and a hole hewed through the fence. While waiting here, I saw an infantry man's leg taken off by a shot, and whirled like a stone through the air, until it came against a caisson with a loud whack."

Overwhelming Confederate counter-battery fire and overwhelming numbers finally forced the Federal gunners off the field. "Our final retreat was executed in the same manner as the advance," Dilger recalled: his men covered Wheeler's and Wheeler's covered his.

Despite the Confederate advantage in elevation, the Federal line between the Mummasburg and Carlisle Roads held their own for a number of hours.

The downfall of the XI Corps—in fact, the downfall of the entire Federal line on July 1, 1863—started along the corps' right flank, much as it had at Chancellorsville.

Oak Hill clearly dominates the plain north of Gettysburg. (dw)

On the Gettysburg Plain

Today, the McClean farm is owned by the National Park Service and is a private residence for one of their staff members. (dw)

Oak Hill, to the northwest, stands 130 feet high—roughly the same height as the famed Willis Hill sector of Marye's Heights at Fredericksburg. Artillery shells from the hill and the Samuel Cobean farm on the Carlisle Road slammed into the ground around near where you are standing.

The large red barn at the base of Oak Hill was owned by Moses McClean, a prominent local attorney and former United States congressman who was renting his farm to David H. Beams at the time of the battle. Beams was not at the farm, though; he was actually serving on the Virginia Peninsula in the 165th Pennsylvania Infantry. Harriet Beams, David's wife, and their three-year-old daughter were at the farm at the time of the battle and fled the area. By the time they returned, all of their possessions had either been stolen or destroyed.

One of the most famous human-interest stories of the battle took place at the McClean farm. Captain Francis Irsch led four companies of the 45th New York towards the barn, where they captured a number of men from the 5th Alabama Infantry. As the prisoners were taken to the rear, Cpl. Rudolph Schwarz of the 45th NY recognized one of the prisoners: his brother. The two men embraced, not having seen one another since they left Germany years earlier. This would be the last time the brothers saw one another, though. Rudolph returned to the front and was killed in action later that day.

On September 14, 1887, members of Dilger's battery came to the Gettysburg battlefield to dedicate three monuments/markers. Their main monument here along West Howard Ave. marks the battery's relative position on the field. Initially deployed to the rear of the monument, closer to the modern homes and buildings along the north side of Gettysburg College, the battery leapfrogged from that area with Wheeler's battery towards Oak Hill. The two units eventually came online just forward of their modern day monuments.

Dilger's other two markers are along the Carlisle Road and in Soldiers' National Cemetery.

Dilger lost 14 men and 24 horses and had one gun disabled. Dilger went on to complain that the ammunition was faulty. "I was completely dissatisfied with the results observed with the fuses for the 12-pounder shells and spherical case, on the explosion of which, by the most careful preparation, you cannot depend," he groused. "The fuses for the 3-inch ammunition caused a great many explosions in our front right before the mount of the guns. . . ." Soldiers referred to the phenomenon as "rotten shot."

Later in the war, Dilger's battery was transferred to the Western Theater where, as popular legend has had it, they had the distinction of being the battery that fired the shot that killed Confederate Lt. Gen. Leonidas Polk. "The Fighting Bishop" as he was known, because he was the Episcopal bishop of Louisiana, was one of the most controversial figures in the Confederacy.

A small monument to the advanced position of the 45th New York sits along the lane to the McClean farm. (cm)

The monument next in line to Dilger's is one to Wheeler's 13th New York Battery, which consisted of four 3-inch ordinance rifles. Wheeler was a 26-year-old Yale-trained lawyer who came to his country's call in 1861. Wheeler recalled withdrawing from this battery line: "While crossing the fields, one of my guns was dismounted by a shot, and, after making the greatest efforts to get it off, I was obliged to leave it on the ground; but on the 5th of July, when we took possession of the entire field of battle, I went down with my blacksmith, mended the carriage, and brought the gun off in triumph." In all, Wheeler lost 13 men wounded or missing (four wounded severely), 12 horses, and one gun that was dismounted. Wheeler did not survive the war; he was killed in action during the 1864 Atlanta campaign.

➔ TO STOP 10

Continue on Howard Avenue. Ahead of you is the intersection of Howard Avenue and the Biglerville Road (Route 34). Proceed straight through the stop sign. Ahead of you is the knoll occupied by Francis Barlow's division during the fighting on the First Day. There is ample parking along Howard Avenue.

GPS: 39 50.726 N, 77 13.586 W

Collapse

CHAPTER TEN

JULY 1 1863

At midafternoon, history began to repeat itself.

The XI Corps, deployed across the Gettysburg plain, anchored its right flank on a small knoll near the Harrisburg Road, which came into the town from the north. Barlow's Knoll, as it would come to be known, would take its name from Brig. Gen. Francis C. Barlow, whose brigade consisted of men from New York, Pennsylvania, Connecticut, and Ohio.

Barlow himself had come by way of Harvard from New York, where he'd been practicing law and occasionally writing for the New York *Tribune*. He enlisted for the war in its first month—and just a single day after getting married. His boyish looks made him look "like a highly independent mounted newsboy," said one officer, but Barlow earned a reputation as a dependable fighter and rose steadily through the ranks. By the time he'd found himself a brigadier general, he'd taken to wearing a red-checkered shirt into battle beneath his unbuttoned uniform jacket.

His assignment to the XI Corps had been a mixed blessing. He'd been "seduced" into taking the higher command responsibility, but he loathed most of his men. "[T]hese Dutch won't fight," he grumbled. "Their officers say so & they say so themselves & they ruin all with whom they come in contact." He made it known to anyone who would listen that his brigade had been on detached duty on May 2 at Chancellorsville and so had played no role in the corps' disastrous collapse.

History—and Barlow himself—would rectify that shortly.

Originally deployed close to the north edge of town, Barlow took it upon himself to move his men forward. He believed the knoll, a few hundred yards in advance

Today, a statue to Francis Barlow stands on the knoll that bears his name, as though staking a proud claim to the piece of ground that was the source of such trouble in 1863 and such controversy ever since. (dd)

A monument to the 17th Connecticut sits on Barlow's Knoll among the four cannon that mark the position of the 4th U.S. Artillery, Battery G. The commander of the 17th Connecticut, Lt. Col. Douglas Fowler, was killed moments after telling his men, "Dodge the big ones, boys." (loc)

Francis Barlow looked like a boy general, but the brigadier was actually 28 years old. (loc)

of the rest of the XI Corps' line, offered an advantage in elevation that counterbalanced its relative isolation. "I had an admirable position," Barlow later said. "The country was an open one for a long distance around and could be swept by our artillery."

Barlow's unauthorized movement stymied his superiors. "I had ordered General Barlow to refuse his right wing," Gen. Schurz wrote later, "that is . . . to use it against a possible flanking movement by the enemy."

Thus far, all the action had been to Barlow's left and west. The secure spot on the knoll would allow him to defend against anything that came from that direction.

And then Jubal Early showed up.

* * *

Robert E. Lee's "Bad Old Man" had last been in Gettysburg five days earlier, on June 26, when his men routed the state militia sent to guard the town. After that brief first battle of Gettysburg, Early's column had swept eastward to York where they stood on the banks of the Susquehanna River, then northward towards Harrisburg. They never made it that far. Recalled by Ewell following Lee's order to concentrate, Early had marched as far as Heidlersburg before camping for the night on June 30. Expressing no real rush, Ewell ordered Early to resume the march by 8:00 a.m.

Only as Early's men neared the field around 2:00 p.m. did messages urge them forward toward the sounds of battle—"the sullen roar of musketry and cannon," one of Early's staffers recalled, "the mechanical 'Hip, hip! hurrah!' of the Federal infantry . . . the clear, sonorous, hearty soul-stirring ring of the Confederate cheer."

The Harrisburg Road brought Early's division into position about three-quarters of a mile to the left of Rodes' division, which had, by then, taken just about all the abuse it could.

Using a ridgeline for cover, Early deployed his men on high ground in Barlow's front and then ordered Gordon's brigade forward. Gordon "drew his sword, the Georgians grasped their arms, and in a few minutes the line was moving through a field of yellow wheat like a dark gray wave in a sea of gold," one observer said.

"Then came one of the most warlike and animated spectacles I ever looked upon," a Confederate officer recalled.

The brigades of Brig. Gen. Harry Hays and Col. Isaac Avery followed Gordon's advance. Early's fourth brigade, Brig. Gen. William "Extra Billy" Smith, deployed to the east to cover the division's flank, which also served as the left flank of the entire army. In particular, Early ordered Smith to keep an eye on the York Road in case any Union cavalry appeared there—a directive that would have important repercussions later.

The Confederate line stretched for a mile, one Federal guessed. Its ends extended past either end of Barlow's position. Worse, Barlow's advanced position from the rest of the XI Corps created a salient—a portion of the line that bulged out. This let the Confederate attackers wrap around it and attack Barlow's position from multiple sides. "[W]ith the enemy in front and flank," one Ohio officer lamented, they were exposed "to an enfilading fire of the most terrible kind."

Rather than retreat, Barlow ordered a counterattack, but his men found themselves too outmatched and their position untenable. "[I]t was a fearful slaughter," one Confederate contended, "the golden wheat fields, a few minutes before in beauty, now gone, and the ground covered with the dead and wounded in blue."

It was "a violent and bruising struggle," said one soldier, but eventually the Federals gave way. "Away went guns and knapsack, and they fled for dear life," a Union surgeon observed.

Brig. Gen. John Brown Gordon's memoirs serve as one of the most colorful, if exaggerated, accounts of the Civil War. (loc)

Barlow, trying to rally his men, went down when a bullet hit him in the left side. When a pair of his men tried to help him from the field, one of them was killed; the other abandoned Barlow. Too weak to go on, Barlow collapsed as Confederates flooded past him.

Other pockets of resistance likewise collapsed. The men "looked more like animals than human beings," recalled one of Barlow's subordinates, Col. Wladimir Krzyanowski, who said that "the portrait of battle was the portrait of hell."

By 3:30 p.m., the entire Federal position crumbled, "falling back with little or no regularity, regimental organizations having become destroyed," said Brig. Gen. Adelbert Ames, another of Barlow's subordinates.

"The whole of that portion of the Union army in my front was in inextricable confusion and in flight," wrote Gordon, whose brigade captured some 1,800

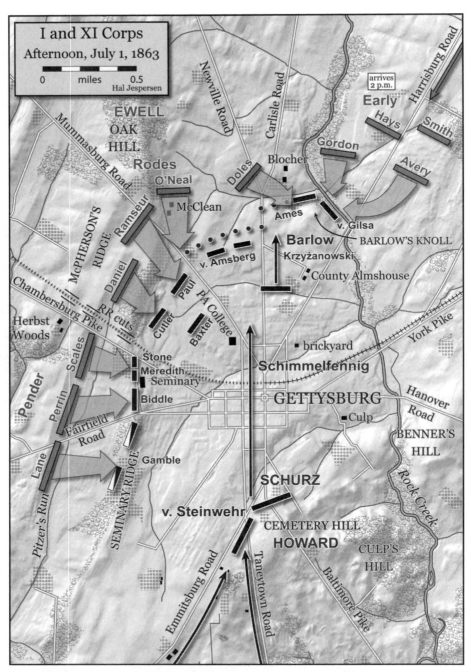

I AND XI CORPS—Pressure from the west forced the Federal I Corps to fall back to a consolidated position along Seminary Ridge. However, an attack against the right flank of the XI Corps triggered the crumble of the entire Federal line. To help cover the retreat, Schurz sent reinforcements into the town, but they were soon overwhelmed.

prisoners—impressive considering that Gordon went into battle with only 1,813 men of his own.

The retreat of the Eleventh Corps, fleeing in disorganized disgrace, might have been Chancellorsville all over again.

* * *

To the west of town, Confederate Maj. Gen. Henry Heth—the man ordered not to bring on a general engagement—was pounding hard at Abnder Doubleday's I Corps line.

"Hold out, if possible, a little longer," Howard had told Doubleday, but Doubleday was finding out just how hard that was. His exhausted troops had been force-marched to the battlefield and then thrown into battle against a foe that was outflanking them on both sides.

To buy time, Doubleday directed an orderly withdrawal from McPherson ridge to a more consolidated position back on Seminary Ridge. They did so "under a murderous fire," one Michigander said. From the Confederate perspective, the sight looked "as merry as a marriage bell." Federals threw up a hasty barricade to assist in their defense.

Confederates took the opportunity to reform as well, and a new division—Maj. Gen. William Dorsey Pender's—swept forward.

At some point during the fighting, Federals noticed that their counterparts to the north were falling back. It wasn't readily apparent if they were withdrawing, retreating, collapsing—just that the "saucy battle-flags of the Confederacy" were sweeping townward in their wake.

With no support on their right flank, and with Confederates now pressing them there, the I Corps had no choice but to pull out. Some soldiers just up and left, "each to care for himself through the town," one solder said. Another described it as lacking any "semblance of military order with every man for himself and the Rebs take the hindmost."

Doubleday did his best to maintain order, though and all things considered, he demonstrated credible skill at getting his men off the field—but he would get no credit for it. Behind the lines, the Federal commander responsible for overseeing events was Oliver Otis Howard, who still bore the shame of his XI Corps'

The 82nd Illinois was reportedly the last Union regiment to fall back into town. (cm)

The fight along Seminary Ridge, said one South Carolinian, changed "the halls of learning into a scene of bloodshed and carnage." (loc)

A walking trail across from the Seminary Museum allows visitors to explore the Federal fallback position on Seminary Ridge (see Epilogue). (cm)

collapse at Chancellorsville and who had just seen them collapse again. In an effort to exonerate his own men and save himself further humiliation, the one-armed general would be quick to cast blame at Doubleday for the day's reverses.

And even now, the man most frequently blamed for the collapse of the Union army at Chancellorsville was ensconced on Cemetery Hill south of Gettysburg, in the perfect position to prevent another.

At Barlow's Knoll

Blocher's Knoll is better known today as Barlow's Knoll, taking its name from the XI Corps division commander. Today, four cannon sit atop the knoll representing the 4th U.S. Artillery, Battery G. At the time of the battle, the battery had six guns, but two of them had been placed in position near the Almshouse, leaving only four to defend the knoll itself.

Commanding the battery was Lt. Bayard Wilkeson. After an enemy shell tore his leg to pieces, Wilkeson calmly applied a tourniquet and amputated his own limb while still on the field. When the fighting had subsided, Wilkeson was carried to the Almshouse, which had been turned into a makeshift hospital. Late that evening, suffering from pain and thirst, Wilkeson asked for water. As a full canteen was placed in his hand, an enlisted man nearby made the same request. Wilkeson selflessly handed the man his canteen; by the time the soldier finished his drink, Wilkeson had expired.

The wounded Francis Barlow, meanwhile, was abandoned by his own men. He survived his injury and returned to the army as a division commander in Maj. Gen. Winfield Scott Hancock's II Corps. As John Brown Gordon liked to tell the tale, he came upon Barlow shortly after his opponent had collapsed on the battlefield. Gordon offered succor and promised to carry a message to Barlow's wife. Making sure Barlow made it into the hands of medical personnel, Gordon rode off to rejoin the battle.

Years later, Gordon supposedly ran into Barlow at a dinner in Washington, D.C. Assuming that Barlow could not have survived his wound and thinking that he was meeting one of his relatives, Gordon inquired "Are you related to the Barlow who was killed at Gettysburg?"

"Why I am the man sir!" replied Barlow, who had also assumed that Gordon had not survived the war. "Are you related to the Gordon who killed me?"

"I am the man, sir" Gordon responded.

Gordon later wrote that "no words of mine can convey any conception of the emotions awakened by those startling announcements." The two reportedly became fast friends and repeated versions of the story for years thereafter. Modern historians doubt the veracity of the story, however, because Barlow's men and Gordon's squared off directly against each other in the Wilderness in May of 1864. It's unlikely that such a fight could have happened without the commanders discovering the identity of their opponents.

The Barlow statue, dedicated by the state of New York on June 6, 1922, was designed by sculptor John Massey Rhind, who also created the Gettysburg statues for Alexander Webb, Abner Doubleday, and John Robinson. (cm)

⟶ TO STOP 11

Continue along Howard Avenue over Barlow's Knoll and proceed to the stop sign at the intersection of Howard Avenue and the Old Harrisburg Road (Business Route 15). Turn right onto Old Harrisburg Road and proceed 0.5 miles. At the intersection of the Old Harrisburg Road and East Lincoln Avenue, bear right onto East Lincoln Avenue and then make an immediate left onto North Stratton Street. Proceed on North Stratton Street for 0.1 miles and turn left onto Coster Avenue. Proceed to the end of Coster Avenue. Much of the surrounding area is private property; please respect the owners' rights when parking.

GPS 39 50.106 N, 77 13.666 W

At the base of Barlow Knoll, visitors will see the Almshouse Cemetery, which still serves as the final resting place for many of the almshouse's former occupants. (cm)

Battle in the Brickyard

CHAPTER ELEVEN

JULY 1 1863

Atop Cemetery Hill, tired men from Pennsylvania and New York lounged about the tombstones and tried to get a bite to eat. The marble and granite markers seemed to stare at them as if delivering an omen. Munching on hardtack, they tried to shrug it off, but the echoes of musketry and artillery made the message tough to ignore.

Trailing the rest of the XI Corps, these men of the 27th and 73rd Pennsylvania and the 134th and 154th New York had arrived at Gettysburg that afternoon. They were part of Brig. Gen. Adolph von Steinwehr's division. Rather than deploying for battle, though, the brigade had been placed in reserve just south of Gettysburg. Their position in and below Evergreen Cemetery could not have been less auspicious. Waiting anxiously, the men stacked arms and watched. In the distance, to the north and northwest, gray lines closed on their comrades.

With Confederates bearing down on Barlow's division and the Union line about to break, a rider arrived to summon the brigade to the fight. Led by their commander, Col. Charles Coster, they double-timed through the streets of town to the north, hoping to cover Barlow's retreat.

Fleeing Federals choked the streets around them. A private in the 154th recalled the scene as one of "confusion and disaster."

Major General Carl Schurz was waiting for them. They arrived, Schurz recalled, "[w]hile I was doing my utmost . . . to rally and re-form what was within my reach of the First Division. . . ." He led the brigade out of the town "and ordered it to deploy on the right of the junction of the roads near the railway station." The 73rd Pennsylvania was posted near the depot. Coster's other

A monument to the 154th New York stands in front of a mural that depicts their role in "the Brickyard Fight." (cm)

Col. Charles Coster enlisted as a private shortly after the firing on Fort Sumter, first in the 7th New York Militia and, later, in the 12th U.S. Infantry, where he then earned a commission as a lieutenant. (md)

three regiments moved out Stratton Street and filed into John Kuhn's brickyard. The property offered little cover beyond a split-rail fence.

Coster's men took up their position none too soon. The Confederate brigades of Brig. Gen. Harry Hays and Col. Isaac Avery were quickly approaching. One New Yorker remembered the Confederates "had a battle flag every few rods." The Keystoners and Empire Staters opened on them; their volleys, said one soldier, "did good execution."

Coster's regiments, however, were outnumbered nearly three to one. Hays and Avery moved in, catching the Union troops in a vice. All the while—as Hays remembered—Confederates delivered "well directed volleys" of their own.

The 154th New York, anchoring the middle of Coster's line, was "stubbornly holding their position until we climbed over into their midst," a Confederate attacker recalled. The regiment stood, said one of its junior officers, "firm as the pyramids, fighting with the desperation of a forlorn hope."

But the 134th, positioned on the right, had a tougher time of it. So did the 27th Pennsylvania on the left.

When the order came to retreat, only the Pennsylvanians heard it; the messenger delivering the retreat order was killed before getting to the other regiments. Meanwhile, the Pennsylvanians "raised up like a flock of blackbirds" and fled, one observer said. From there, the situation quickly descended into disaster for Coster's brigade as the Confederate pincers closed in on both sides.

Nearly surrounded, the Federal retreat became a race for survival back through town. Gettysburg's fences and houses hemmed Coster's men as much as the enemy. "The rebel hordes were close behind, and bent on obtaining the colors," said one Federal color bearer, "but they were foiled." Reaching the safety of the reforming Union lines atop Cemetery Hill, the remnants of Coster's brigade rallied.

They could not have known it then, but their brief stand in Kuhn's brickyard had bought enough time for elements of the XI Corps to withdraw from the battlefield. The brigade paid a steep price, though: some 550 casualties, including 300 prisoners. One hundred and seventy-three of those prisoners came from the 154th alone.

The exhausted survivors resumed their old position in the cemetery, awaiting the next Rebel onslaught.

One of the most surprising memorials on the Gettysburg battlefield is tucked away adjacent to Coster Avenue: a mural depicting the fight at the brickyard. Dedicated on July 1, 1988—the 125th anniversary of the battle—the mural was painted by artist Johan Bjurman and its conceiver and designer, artist/historian Mark Dunkelman. In 2001, the mural received a complete restoration thanks to the "Bearss Brigade," a friends group that supports the work of legendary Civil War historian and battlefield guide Ed Bearss.

Dunkelman, the regimental historian for the 154th New York, had an ancestor, John Langhans, who served with the unit later in the war. The 154th was known as the Hardtack Regiment, a name they earned during the army's "Valley Forge winter" in Stafford, Virginia, in 1863. According to Dunkelman, "the men engaged in unscrupulous trading for that army staple with the German members of their brigade."

In front of the mural stands the 154th's granite monument, which was erected by the state of New

Mark Dunkelman (right) stands with Ed Bearss and a pair of young reenactors at the rededication of the Coster Ave. mural in 2001. (md)

The 27th Pennsylvania erected a monument on Cemetery Hill to commemorate its role in fighting there on July 2—but later, the veterans moved it to Coster Avenue to commemorate the regiment's role in the Brickyard fight on July 1 (top). When the state of Pennsylvania appropriated more money for each regiment, the veterans erected a second monument at the original Cemetery Hill location (bottom). (dd, cm)

York and dedicated in 1890. Coster Avenue also holds an eagle-topped monument to the 27th Pennsylvania, dedicated in 1884. The 27th has a larger second monument, dedicated in 1889, on Cemetery Hill.

The fate of the colors of Coster's brigade is clouded in confusion. Presumably the color bearers of the 27th Pennsylvania made it safely back to the main Federal line, flags in hand. In the 134th New York, Sgt. John Carroll carried the national flag. When the regiment was driven from the brickyard, the soldier carrying the 134th's state flag was killed. Another picked it up and was wounded, whereupon Carroll grabbed it. Now carrying both flags, Carroll was also wounded. But before being taken prisoner, he wrapped the state flag around his body, hiding it beneath his sack coat. He remained in Confederate custody for three days before being left behind when Lee's army withdrew. Thus he reunited the state flag with his regiment, making him, according to one account, "as happy as a king."

When Carroll fell, Capt. Matthew Cheney of the 154th New York picked up the 134th's national flag and carried it to safety. In the postwar years, however, Cheney stated he rescued both flags of the 134th. In the 154th New York, the color bearers carrying the national and state flags were both mortally wounded. First Sgt. James Bird rescued the state flag. A postwar account stated a member of the 134th saved the 154th's national flag, but immediately after the battle several members of the 154th reported it was lost. However, neither Hays nor Avery or their regimental commanders reported capturing colors in the brickyard fight, as was customary in after action reports. Whether the 154th's national flag was captured or not remains a mystery.

→ TO STOP 11A

Turn around and proceed back to North Stratton Street. Make a left on North Stratton Street and proceed 0.2 miles. As you cross the railroad, you will notice the Gettysburg Fire Department on your left. Near the fire department parking lot, next to the tracks, you will see the Amos Humiston monument. Park on North Stratton Street and walk to the monument. Due to emergency vehicles entering and leaving the fire department, please exercise caution.

GPS 39 49.921 N, 77 13.722 W

→ TO STOP 12

Continue on North Stratton Street for 450 feet to the intersection of North Stratton Street and Route 30 East. Turn left onto Route 30 East. Up ahead at the first traffic light, bear right onto Hanover Street (Route 116). Proceed 0.9 miles and turn right onto Benner's Hill. There is ample parking along Benner's Hill..

GPS 39 49.658 N, 77 12.821 W

A monument for Amos Humiston—the only monument on the battlefield dedicated to a single soldier—sits along North Stratton Avenue. His story is told in Appendix E. (cm)

Brig. Gen. Adolph von Steinwehr (left) might have faded entirely into obscurity after the battle of Gettysburg—except one of the most popular tourist areas in town sprung up along the street that bears his name (right), making it one of the battle of Gettysburg's most unusual legacies. (loc; cm)

CHAPTER TWELVE
JULY 1 1863

At around five o'clock, Richard Ewell rode into the center of Gettysburg, his staff surrounding him. He didn't know the particulars, but he certainly didn't like what he could see. "It was now within an hour & a half of dark," wrote Ewell's chief-of-staff, his stepson, Campbell Brown. "[T]he enemy's force on the hill already showed a larger front than the combined lines of our two Divisions—they were a mile & a quarter away."

On the way into town, Ewell had run into Gordon, who urged his commander to press the attack forward to Cemetery Hill. In town, Ewell received similar advice from Hays. He also received orders from Lee, courtesy of Capt. James Power Smith and then, moments later, from one of Lee's staffer's, Walter Taylor.

Lee's orders had been for Ewell to attack if he "could do so to advantage," Smith later recounted. Taylor's postwar writings say that Lee "could see the enemy retreating over those hills, without organization and in great confusion, that it was only necessary to press 'those people' in order to secure possession of the heights, and that, if possible, [Lee] wished [Ewell] to do this."

Ewell determined he could make the attack, but he wanted support from Hill's Third Corps. He sent Smith back to Lee with his request, then he ordered Early and Rodes to get into position.

But Smith soon returned bearing word from Lee: Hill had no men to lend in support of the attack. The Third Corps had been handled badly in its victory over the Federal I Corps, so Hill chose to rest his weary men rather than continue to press the attack—even though he had a full division, under Maj. Gen. Richard Anderson, that had remained out of the fight entirely.

Ewell was to carry Cemetery Hill alone, if possible—

Artillery on Benner's Hill played a particularly important role on July 2. (dd)

William Smith, a two-time governor of Virginia, acquired his nickname "Extra Billy" under President Andrew Jackson. Smith, then serving as a postal contractor, received a salary based upon the number of miles traveled. To increase his pay, Smith ordered his stagecoaches to travel longer routes or "extra" miles. At the time of Gettysburg, he was governor-elect of Virginia, serving in that post for the second time. His first term had been during the Mexican-American War in the 1840s. (loc)

but Lee also reiterated his earlier admonition not to bring on a general engagement if at all possible.

Ewell, it seems, was stuck.

Just then, "up came 'Freddy' Smith, son of 'Extra Billy,' to say that a heavy force was reported moving up in their rear," Campbell Brown recalled. "Extra Billy" was governor-elect of Virginia, so even the irascible Jubal Early showed him deference. Ewell did, too.

"General, I don't much believe in this," Early said to Ewell, "but prefer to suspend my movements until I can send & inquire into it."

"Well," Ewell replied, "do so." In the meantime, he planned to get Rodes into position and also try to prod action out of Hill.

Early responded by sending Gordon's entire brigade to join Smith's along the York Road. Ewell, worried about a threat on his flank even as he prepared for a frontal assault, chose to take a look for himself. He and his officers rode to the top of Benner's Hill. They saw a line of skirmishers they first mistook for Federals but, as it turned out, were actually men sent out earlier in the day by Smith. The coast was clear, it seemed. Early said Smith had filed "an unfounded report."

Unbeknownst to them, though, Brig. Gen. Alpheus Williams of the Federal XII Corps saw the mounted Confederate officers on the hilltop, "evidently reconnoitering."

Not seeing any signs of artillery or any large force, Williams directed one of his subordinates, Brig. Gen. Thomas Ruger, "to deploy his brigade, under cover of the woods, and charge the hill, supported by the 1st Brigade under Col. McDougall. I had with me two batteries of artillery, which were put in the road, and directed to follow the assault, come into battery on the rest of the hill, and open on the enemy's masses."

Federal soldiers followed an old Revolutionary War-era trail through the woods to the pike. "[T]he corps was moved to the right across country east of Rock Creek, until it faced a slope toward Benner's Hill, where the line was halted and deployed with skirmishers in front," wrote the colonel of the 2nd Massachusetts Infantry. "The country here was open, and mounted officers of the enemy could be seen on the high ground apparently examining the position."

Ruger's brigade was actually ascending the slope of the hill, Williams said, when he received orders to withdraw the division toward the Baltimore Pike and take position for the night. The time, he said, was sometime between five-thirty and six o'clock.

Ever after, Jubal Early insisted that "Extra Billy" Smith had been seeing things along the York Pike. But, to be safe, Early kept Gordon and Smith along the York

Pike all night, tying up valuable men from making any assault on Cemetery Hill.

But it's likely that Smith did indeed see something—elements of the Twelfth Corps coming onto the field at precisely the right moment to serve as a much-needed distraction. "The appearance of the division in this position at the time it occurred," said Ruger in his official report, "was apparently a timely diversion in favor of our forces, as the farther advance of the enemy ceased."

Maj. Gen. Edward "Allegheny" Johnson was called "Old Clubby" by his men because of a hickory walking stick he used, necessitated by a foot wound he'd received at the battle of McDowell as part of Stonewall Jackson's 1862 Valley Campaign. (loc)

*   *   *

While Ewell's reconnaissance failed to turn up hard proof of the Federal threat, it did lead to another vital discovery: Culp's Hill sat unoccupied a quarter of a mile to the southeast of Cemetery Hill. Ewell knew he could avoid assaulting Cemetery Hill entirely if his men could occupy Culp's Hill, which would make the Union position on Cemetery Hill untenable.

Ewell suggested to Early that his men occupy Culp's Hill. Early balked. His men "had been doing all the hard marching and fighting and was not in condition to make the move," "Old Jube" groused. Instead, he passed the buck to Ewell's third division, that of Maj. Gen. Edward "Allegheny" Johnson. Johnson's men, approaching the battlefield via a route farther west than the rest of the Second Corps in order to protect the corps' wagon train, found themselves snarled in a traffic jam along the Chambersburg Pike, entangling them with the First and Third Corps.

Johnson had arrived ahead of his men, though. Hearing Early shrug off responsibility, Johnson traded sharp words with him, but Ewell took Early's side.

By the time Johnson's men arrived, Federal soldiers had already occupied the hill. A 30-man squad from the 42nd Virginia, sent by Johnson to reconnoiter, wound up as Federal prisoners.

The opportunity to take the ground without a fight had slipped away.

With the foliage down, it's easy to see the observation tower on Culp's Hill, some 1400 yards away, from Benner's Hill. (cm)

At Benner's Hill

The various movements of Brig. Gen. Alpheus Williams (above) on the Confederate left flank worried Brig. Gen. "Extra Billy" Smith enough that Smith's superior, Maj. Gen. Jubal Early, committed two full brigades to cover the eastern approaches to town. (loc)

Benner's Hill offers one the best and most-impressive views of Gettysburg. Cemetery and Culp's Hills are less than 2,000 yards away—close enough that one can make out the monuments on Cemetery Hill. Directly to the west is the cupola of the Lutheran Seminary.

On July 1, Brig. Gen. Alpheus Williams' division of Maj. Gen. Henry Slocum's XII Corps came within a breath of taking this high ground. The defeat of the XI Corps made the position untenable for Williams, and he was forced to withdraw to the new Union line forming south of town. Second Corps commander Richard Ewell finally came out here with a small gaggle of subordinates to scope out the situation for himself, and in the end, he decided Smith's worries were groundless. Ironically, Williams himself saw Ewell's party.

Williams' inability to occupy Benner's Hill left the elevation in Confederate hands, making it an ideal artillery position for the engagement the following day. The position, however, had its drawbacks. Benner's Hill appears much as it did in 1863; thus, the open terrain exposed the gray artillery crews to fire from Union batteries on East Cemetery Hill. It was, said one cannoneer, "simply a hell infernal."

➤ TO STOP 12A

Return to Route 116 and turn left. Proceed 2.2 miles to the Diamond. Bear right in the Diamond until you reach Baltimore Street (Route 15 Business), which will be the third exit. Proceed on Baltimore Street for 0.25 miles. After you pass Breckenridge Street on your right, park along the street. The Garlach house is marked with a sign.

GPS: N 39.82622 W 77.23116

➤ TO STOP 13

Proceed on Baltimore Street for 0.15 miles to the traffic light at the intersection of Baltimore Street and von Steinwehr Avenue. Go straight at the light to continue on Baltimore Street. You will now begin your ascent of Cemetery Hill. At the crest of the hill on the right is the entrance to the Soldiers' National Cemetery. Beyond it is the entrance to Gettysburg's Evergreen Cemetery. Directly across from the entrances to these cemeteries is the Union position on Cemetery Hill. There is parking along the right of Baltimore Street. Be sure to exercise caution when crossing Baltimore Street.

GPS: 39 49.269 N, 77 13.753 W

In the chaotic Union retreat through Gettysburg, Brig. Gen. Alexander Schimmelfennig (top) became trapped between the side streets and onrushing Confederate troops. With his horse shot from under him, Schimelfennig, rather than surrender, made his way through the backyards of houses until he reached the Garlach property that bordered Baltimore Street. There, he hid himself from the swarming Rebels by taking shelter in a culvert. Even after darkness set in, he deemed it too dangerous to risk moving from his hiding place to the new Union lines atop Cemetery Hill. Making contact with Mrs. Catherine Garlach (middle), the lady of the house supplied the general with food on July 2. Mrs. Garlach also sensed the danger posed by the Confederates and did not venture into her yard for the remainder of the battle. Miraculously, Schmmelfennig went unnoticed by the Confederates the entire time. It was not until the enemy had abandoned Gettysburg on July 4 did he emerge from hiding. Over time, the legend evolved that Schimmelfenning took refuge in a pig sty—perhaps shaped by the indignity of his situation and prejudices against the "Flying Dutchmen" of the XI Corps. (There was a slop bucket and a woodshed in the yard, but no sty [bottom].) Schimmelfenning would survive the war only to die of tuberculosis in the fall of 1865.
(loc)(achs)(achs)(dd)

Cemetery Hill
CHAPTER THIRTEEN
JULY 1 1863

Oliver Otis Howard didn't know what the German was saying, but the tone was unmistakable. The bedraggled colonel and his men had begun filtering out from between the houses on the south edge of town and up the slope of Cemetery Hill, defeat heavy in their bones. Howard watched them approach.

"Sergeant, plant your flag down here in the stone wall," he called to the regiment's color-bearer.

"All right," the exhausted man replied, "if you will go with me, I will!"

The one-armed general scooped up the flag, crossed to the stone wall, and leaned the flag there. The regiment coalesced around it.

Howard turned to another returning regiment. Again, he challenged them to rally. The men "advanced to the stone wall in rear of the village & remained a few moments there," a member of the regiment said. Howard coolly challenged them again, and the men "again advanced to a rail fence still further to the front."

Howard's example "taught me what a cool and confident man could do," said one Federal staff officer. "No hurry, no confusion in his mind. He knew that if he could get his troops in any kind of order back of those stone walls the country was safe, and that upon the succeeding days Lee would meet his great defeat."

Howard's decision to play it safe had paid off.

*   *   *

The headquarters marker of Maj. Gen. Oliver Otis Howard stands only a few hundred feet away from his equestrian statue on Cemetery Hill. (cm)

Even as survivors from the collapsing lines made their way up the northern face of Cemetery Hill, a new arrival to the battlefield was making his way up the southern slope. Major General Winfield Scott Hancock,

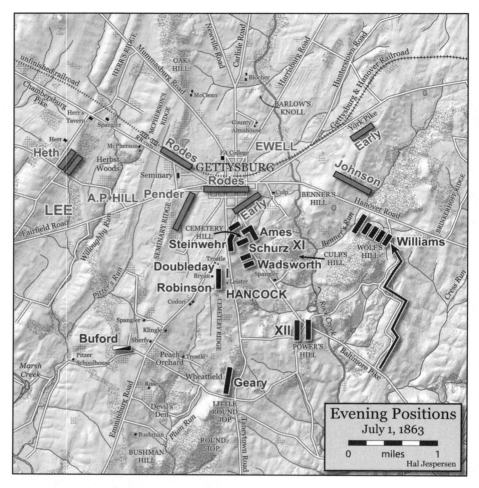

EVENING POSITIONS—The heights south of town provided excellent ground for the overwhelmed Federals to regroup. While Confederates had the opportunity to position themselves on the Federal right flank, early arriving elements of the XII Corps made such a proposition tenuous, so the Confederates held back. The arrival of the entire XII Corps allowed Federals to consolidate the entire position for the night, with more reinforcements scheduled to arrive by morning.

38 years old, was George Gordon Meade's hand-picked emissary to the battlefield. Howard outranked Hancock by a mere 20 days, but Hancock held Meade's confidence in a way Howard didn't.

An 1844 graduate of West Point, Hancock's 19-year career in the military included stints in the Mexican War and the Seminole War. During the early years of the Civil War, he served with such distinction that he earned the nom-de-guerre "Hancock the Superb." He saw especially hard fighting at Antietam's Bloody Lane and in front of Fredericksburg's Stone Wall. At Chancellorsville, his division covered the army's withdrawal after its lines collapsed on May 3. When II Corps commander Maj. Gen. Darius Couch resigned in protest over Hooker's mismanagement of that battle, Hancock was tapped to take Couch's place.

It was 4:30 p.m., and the top of Cemetery Hill was abuzz with barely contained chaos. Hancock began issuing orders for the deployment of troops even before he found Howard. He was "all excitement— not nervous—looking in a thousand ways every minute and giving directions . . . carefully and precisely," one observer noted. Howard, by contrast, directed action "with as much coolness as

Union troops fled pell-mell through the streets of Gettysburg in their retreat, but officers tried to restore some sense of order and organization. (cm)

though he was watching a Fourth of July parade."

"That Glorious Fourth," as it would come to be called, wouldn't come for another three days. In the meantime, Hancock's arrival certainly represented rain on Howard's parade.

Accounts of their meeting differ wildly. As Hancock recalled it, he merely "assumed the command." As Howard recalled it, "[Hancock] said that General Meade had sent him to represent him on the field." Neither man reported animosity, and Howard even recollected the exchange of "a few friendly words between us."

Abner Doubleday, whom Howard would throw under the proverbial streetcar for the collapse of the line, remembered the exchange through bitter hindsight. "Why, Hancock, you cannot give any orders here!" a peevish Howard allegedly barked. "I am in command and I outrank you!"

Even so, Hancock carried written orders in his pocket from Meade, although, to his credit, he seems to have kept them tucked tactfully away.

Perhaps Carl Schurz recalled it most accurately. When Hancock presented himself and his orders from Meade, Howard was flustered but accepted the news professionally. "Howard, in spite of his heart-sore, cooperated so loyally with Hancock that it would have been hard to tell which of the two was the commander and which the subordinate," Schurz said.

Howard settled the XI Corps into place, and Hancock the I Corps. Hancock's "imperious and defiant bearing heartened us all," one Mainer said.

*   *   *

The view from Cemetery Hill toward the east (cm)

Federal artillerists still stand ready on one of Cemetery Hill's monuments. (cm)

Some time around 7:00 p.m., XII Corps commander Maj. Gen. Henry Slocum arrived on the field. His lead elements, which had spooked "Extra Billy" Smith on the Confederate left, added much-needed heft to the "woefully thin" Federal line. Only 7,000 survivors from the I and XI Corps manned the hilltop.

Slocum himself had resisted Howard's repeated calls for backup earlier in the day, preferring instead to get his orders through official channels—which of course wasn't going to happen because Meade had been waiting for an update from Hancock.

Hancock hadn't had time to file a report until 5:25 p.m.—an hour after reaching the field. "I think we will be all right until night," he wrote to Meade. Overall, he worried about the position's flank, but Slocum's movements began to allay that fear. "When night comes, it can be better told what had best be done. I think we can retire; if not, we can fight here, as the ground appears not unfavorable with good troops."

As the situation continued to stabilize, though, Hancock began to appreciate Howard's choice of ground even more. He declared it "the strongest position by nature upon which to fight a battle that I ever saw," and he sent word to Meade to come to the front and see for himself.

Ironically, perhaps apocryphally, a sign hung on the Evergreen Cemetery gatehouse: "Persons caught using firearms in the cemetery will be prosecuted to the fullest extent of the law." Established in 1854, the cemetery remains in operation today. (cm)(loc)

Gettysburg, it seemed, was destined to see more battle.

As dusk settled over the field, Hancock took a seat on one of the stone walls Howard had asked his men to fortify. Carl Schurz joined him. Both men still worried about the Confederates in front of them, ready to spring, but they felt buoyed by the stream of reinforcements filing in behind them.

As their insignia, the men of Schurz's XI Corps wore a crescent moon. Now, as they laid down to rest among the tombstones, wrapped in their cloaks, a full moon rose over them. "There was profound stillness in the graveyard, broken by no sound but the breathing of the men," Schurz recalled, "and here and there the tramp of

a horse's foot; and the sullen rumblings mysteriously floating on the air from a distance all around."

On Cemetery Hill

Some of the stone walls that were so instrumental in Cemetery Hill's defense still criss-cross the crest of the hill. Walking paths meander across the landscape, too.

The eastward view from Cemetery Hill offers an excellent perspective of Culp's Hill. Confederate occupation of the Culp's Hill would have made the Federal position here untenable. Hancock's decision to send the Iron Brigade to Culp's Hill remains one of the most important unsung decisions of the battle. "[I]t was just the thing to do," Howard later affirmed. Doubleday, however, balked, earning a bark from Hancock. "I want you to understand that I am in command here," Hancock snapped. "Send every man you have."

The plot is dominated by the equestrian statues to Winfield Scott Hancock and Oliver Otis Howard. In his book *Gettysburg—The First Day*, the former chief historian of Gettysburg National Military Park, Harry Pfanz, makes an astute observation about the statues. "Hancock's is one of the most dynamic memorials on the field," Pfanz says. Howard's by contrast, "stands with all four hooves planted firmly, as if it and its rider

A myth has grown around all the equestrian statutes at Gettysburg. The story goes that if a horse has one foot off the ground, the rider was wounded during the battle; if it has two feet off the ground, the officer was killed. While this pattern did hold true for many years—as it does with Hancock's statue (left) and Howard's (right)—it was the result of pure coincidence, not intent. Over time, the story developed into such well-accepted battlefield lore that when a statue of Confederate Lt. Gen. James Longstreet was unveiled in 1998 along West Confederate Avenue, outcry arose because the statue "broke" the tradition. In fact, no such tradition ever existed. (cm)

John Buford (seated), pictured with his staff. After their valorous stand on the morning of July 1, Buford's brigades would fight again later in the day. During the last Confederate assault on the I Corps, Gamble's troopers engaged Maj. Gen. William Dorsey Pender's division, while Tom Devin delayed Ewell's march and then helped cover the retreat of the XI Corps. At the end of the day, the exhausted Buford withdrew to a new position south of Gettysburg near a peach orchard that would become famous on July 2. Early that mornng, however, before fighting ever broke out there, Buford received orders to report to Westminster, Maryland, to rest, refit, and protect the army's wagon trains. (loc)

were there to stay." The statues reflect their riders and their leadership styles on July 1, 1863, as well as the controversies still associated with them.

In memorialization, unlike in life, Hancock arrived on Cemetery Hill first. While Hancock spent most of his time during the battle along Cemetery Ridge, Hancock's native state chose to mark the spot where he first appeared on the battlefield. The Commonwealth of Pennsylvania dedicated the statue on June 5, 1896, at a total cost of $30,000. The sculptor, Frank Edwin Ewell, ironically bore the name of the Confederate commander who opposed Federal forces posted on Cemetery Hill. It was the second equestrian statue dedicated on the battlefield (Meade's was first). Maine did not erect its statue to Howard, sculpted by Robert Aitken, until November 12, 1932. "The two statues are separate

entities that seem to ignore each other," Pfanz notes.

Also on the crest of the hill are several artillery monuments. The artillery here late on July 1 played a key part in Hancock's plan for holding the position as the infantry reformed.

Across the street from the equestrian statues is the gatehouse to Evergreen Cemetery. Established in 1854, the cemetery is the final resting place of James Getty, the town's father; Jennie Wade, the only civilian killed

As more and more Federals consolidated on Cemetery Hill, supported by more and more artillery, the position became virtually unassailable—not that Confederates wouldn't try on July 2. (cm)

A seven-foot-tall bronze statue of Elizabeth Thorn, sculpted by Ron Tunison, was dedicated in 2002. It stands not far from the cemetery gatehouse Thorn had called home. (cm)

during the battle; the "Widow Thompson," whose home Robert E. Lee used as his headquarters (as told in the next chapter); and John Burns, a 69-year-old War of 1812 veteran who joined Federal forces on McPherson Ridge (whose story appears in Chapter Four).

Evergreen Cemetery is also the home of the Women's Memorial. The memorial depicts Elizabeth Thorn, six months pregnant, who buried the first 91 soldiers from the battle in Evergreen Cemetery. Thorn's husband, Peter, had been caretaker of the cemetery before enlisting in the 138th Pennsylvania, leaving his wife and three young sons behind to care for the cemetery. With her father's help, she eventually buried 105 bodies in the cemetery. Her baby, carried to term, was born on November 1, 1863; Thorn named her Rose Meade.

The cemetery did not fair well during the battle. "A beautiful cemetery it was, but now is trodden down, laid a waste, desecrated," a Union officer later lamented. "The fences are all down, the many graves have been run over, beautiful lots with iron fences and splendid monuments have been destroyed or soiled, and our infantry and artillery occupy those sacred grounds where the dead are sleeping. It is enough to make one mourn."

Among the notables buried in Evergreen Cemetery are Jennie Wade (top left), John Burns (top right), Mary Thompson (bottom left) and James Getty (bottom right).
(cm, cm, cm, dd)

⟹ **TO STOP 14**

To reach Lee's Headquarters, you must turn around on Baltimore Street. There are a number of places on the right to turn around. Exercise caution when retracing your route. Proceed back toward where you parked to view Tour Stop 13 and continue to the intersection of Baltimore Street and von Steinwehr Avenue. Drive straight through the stoplight 0.4 miles to the intersection of Baltimore Street and West Middle Street. Turn left onto West Middle Street. Proceed 0.7 miles to the intersection of West Middle Street and West Confederate Avenue. To your right will be a street named Seminary Ridge. Turn right onto Seminary Ridge. Exercise caution as you will be driving through the grounds of the Lutheran Theological Seminary. Proceed 0.3 miles to the end of Seminary Ridge until you reach the intersection of Seminary Ridge and Route 30 West. Turn left onto Route 30 West. Up on your immediate right, you will see an entrance to the Quality Inn and Lee's Headquarters. Pull into the parking area marked for Lee's Headquarters.

GPS: 39 50.114 N, 77 14.751 W

E𝑝𝑖𝑙𝑜𝑔𝑢𝑒

Mary Thompson had spent most of the day in her basement as battle raged around her home and through the small apple orchard across the street. The home's thick walls, made of field stone, resisted bullets and artillery shells alike. Her daughter-in-law, Mary, who lived just down the street hunkered in the basement with her. Just the day before, young Mary had given birth to her second child. Now, mother and children and grandmother all huddled, perhaps by lamplight, in the stone house's cellar as the world outside tore itself to pieces.

That morning, Federals had taken up position along McPherson's Ridge, a couple hundred yards to the west of the home—but after a midday lull in the fighting, renewed Confederate attacks pushed the Federals back to Seminary Ridge. The house found itself at the very center of the struggle. "[T]he bullets and shells flew thick and fast," one local resident later said.

After a furious but brief defense, the Federals again drew back, this time through the town to a stronger position atop Cemetery Hill. Their withdrawal left them no opportunity to collect their wounded, though, so the injured, the dying, and the dead lay intermingled in the fields in front of the Lutheran Seminary, in the orchard along the Chambersburg Pike, and in Mrs. Thompson's dooryard.

As soon as the bluecoated troops withdrew and the gray tide swept after them, Mary crept forth from the safety of her stone sanctuary to see what aid she could lend amidst the harvest of death around her.

"The Widow Thompson," as townsfolk called her, had known her share of misfortune during her 69 years. Her first husband, Daniel, died unexpectedly at the age of 30. Her second husband, Joshua, spiraled into

The Confederate flag still flies over Lee's Headquarters. (cm)

The Widow Thompson (above) reportedly said Lee behaved with "gentlemanly deportment . . . whilst in her house," but complained "bitterly of the robbery and general destruction of her goods by some of his attendants." (achs)

The Widow Thompson's home sat along Chambersburg Pike where the road crested Seminary Ridge. (loc)

alcoholism—he was, contested Mary's oldest daughter, a "habitual drunk"—and by 1850 seems to have vanished. Mary was forced to raise her eight children on her own.

"An empty stone house and fenceless yard were all that was left," said one observer, who noted that the widow's "house and lot were filled with wounded and dying."

In the midst of the commotion, a knot of Confederate officers appeared along the Chambersburg Pike. Orders were given. Tents began to spring up in the ruined orchard across from the Widow's house. One of the officers, though, rode his stately gray horse over to the stone house, recognizing not only the shelter it offered but the additional safety, as well.

Robert E. Lee had chosen Widow Thompson's sturdy stone house as his headquarters.

*   *   *

The day had started well for Lee, who was in high spirits as he rode with his army through the gap in the mountains from Chambersburg. But midmorning, as he crested the ridge that would bring him down toward Cashtown, he and his "Old Warhorse," second-in-command Lt. Gen. James Longstreet heard the ominous rumble of artillery in the distance. "This caused Lee some little uneasiness," said one of Lee's staff officers.

The generals might have exchanged a confused glance before Lee spurred on his horse, Traveler, so he could investigate. Lee had ordered his lead elements to avoid any kind of general engagement until the army had concentrated. There should not *be* any sound of artillery.

A. P. Hill's Third Corps led the march, but the Third Corps commander had spent the morning in bed, recovering from yet another of his repeated bouts of illness. He, too, had heard the sound of artillery, as well as the echoes of musketfire, and finally rose from his cot to investigate even as Lee appeared, demanding answers. *I don't know*, Hill admitted—but he volunteered to ride forward and find out.

Lee normally depended on his chief of cavalry, Maj. Gen. James Ewell Brown "Jeb" Stuart, to provide such answers. As it was, Stuart was nowhere to be found. On June 25, he'd left on a mission to wreck havoc behind the marching Union columns as the army moved northward. The ride was similar to his once-vaunted "ride around McClellan" on the Peninsula in the spring of 1862, when he circumnavigated the entire Army of the Potomac, made fools of his Federal counterparts, and grabbed headlines across the North and South. Now, the Federal army, pursuing Lee faster than anticipated, had cut Stuart off and the cavalier was engaged in a desperate struggle to make his way back.

This shot of the Widow Thompson's house was taken shortly after the battle. Thompson can be seen, center, with one of Matthew Brady's assistants. Brady, too, stands there, though is obscured by the foliage. (loc)

Lee knew none of this. "I cannot think of what has become of Stuart," he murmured. "I ought to have heard from him before now. . . . In the absence of reports from him, I am in ignorance as to what we have in front of us here. It may be the whole Federal army." He would articulate the concern repeatedly throughout the day, to almost anyone in earshot.

Lee rode forward and found Hill just as the morning's fight was winding down. At about that time, Campbell Brown—staff officer and stepson of Second Corps commander Richard Ewell—found Lee and reported the corps' situation. By then, Lee's ebullient mood of early morning had dissolved completely. Brown noted "a peculiar searching, almost querulous, impatience" in Lee, who again wondered aloud about Stuart and again impressed "very strongly that a general engagement was to be avoided until the arrival of the rest of the army."

Brown did not reach his stepfather in time to stop Ewell from launching his assaults from Oak Ridge. Meanwhile, Henry Heth, who had started the battle that morning against orders and now looked for redemption, asked for permission to renew his attacks. Lee had, at first, repeated to Heth what he'd said to Brown—in fact, what he'd been saying all along—that Longstreet was not yet up, that the army was not yet concentrated, that he did not want a general engagement.

But what Lee wanted and what unfolded were two separate things.

And as he considered the situation—his men pressing unexpected advantages against an isolated part of the Union army—he allowed the tempest to take him, and he ordered Heth in.

*   *   *

Lee's first report on the battle of Gettysburg, written

on July 4 to Confederate President Jefferson Davis, recalled the action of the day:

> *The two leading divisions of [Hill's and Ewell's] corps, upon reaching the vicinity of Gettysburg, found the enemy and attacked him, driving him from the town, which was occupied by our troops. The enemy's loss was heavy, including more than four thousand prisoners. He took up a strong position in rear of the town which he immediately began to fortify, and here his reinforcements joined him.*

"It is believed that the enemy suffered severely in these operations," Lee wrote, summing up the entire battle but speaking just as well about the first day, "but our own loss has not been light."

Of the 48,000 men engaged on July 1, fully one-third of them ended up killed, wounded, or captured: some 7,000 Confederates casualties and some 9,000 Union casualties. Among the Confederate wounded was Henry Heth, knocked out of action with a head wound.

On the whole, Lee's men had performed well, although subordinate commanders repeatedly failed him throughout the day: Heth's lack of aggressiveness, O'Neal's bungling, Iverson's ineptitude, and Early's peevishness.

But despite the casualties and the mediocre performance of his brigadiers, Lee had scored an unexpected victory on Northern soil—or partial victory, anyway. More work remained, though. Ever the aggressor, Lee looked to finish the task.

*   *   *

Late in the afternoon, Lee's "Old Warhorse," James Longstreet, finally rode into Gettysburg in advance of his corps. The burly Georgian found the headquarters flag posted in the orchard across from a stone house. Seeing that Lee was occupied, though, he took out his binoculars and glassed the terrain, the troops, and the town. In the distance, he could see the Federal army ensconced on a far hilltop.

"We could not call the enemy to position better suited to our plans," Longstreet said when Lee finally called him over. "All we have to do is to file around his left and secure good ground between him and his capital." Longstreet expected Lee to stick with his original intention not "to deliver a general battle so far from our base unless attacked."

Lee surprised him. *No*, the commander indicated, striking the air with his closed fist. "If he is there to-morrow I will attack him," Lee said.

Longstreet hid his alarm. "If he is there to-morrow,"

the First Corps commander said, "it will be because he wants you to attack." That was a good reason for not doing so, he concluded.

But Lee, his dander up, flushed with the day's success, the memory of his recent victory at Chancellorsville fresh in his mind, eyed the Union army south of town. His men had rarely failed to drive the enemy from a position. Today had been a close thing. He had almost beaten "those people."

Tomorrow, he decided, he would.

A headquarters marker for Lee stands in the field across the street from Widow Thompson's house, with McPherson's barn in the background. (cm)

At Lee's Headquarters

The house Mary Thompson lived in was built circa 1833 while the property was owned by a local businessman, Michael C. Clarkson. By 1844, Clarkson ran into financial trouble, and his properties auctioned off. One of his properties, occupied by Mary Thompson, went up for auction in 1846, and one of Clarkson's close associates, Pennsylvania politician Thaddeus Stevens, bought the house and the adjoining three acres for 16 dollars. Stevens was listed as "trustee" of Mary since, legally, married women could not own property in Pennsylvania; Mary's husband, John, although missing, was still alive somewhere. By 1851, after John's death the preceding year, the deed was transferred to Mary's name.

"General Lee's Headquarters" attracted the attention of curious visitors almost immediately after the battle and has remained a popular attraction. (loc)

Speculation has swirled in the century and a half since about the nature of the relationship between Stevens and Mary Thompson. "The speculation . . . has been plentiful, and sometimes a bit melodramatic," says historian Timothy H. Smith in his detailed book *The Story of Lee's Headquarters*. "So much time has now passed since the events surrounding the auction that historians may never know the real story."

The Widow Thompson lived in the house until her death in 1873. In 1896, the interior of the house caught fire, although the exterior remained intact. Insurance money allowed the owner to restore the home, says one account, "in order to preserve a battlefield relic."

The home seems to have then had a less noble use.

In advance of the 75th anniversary of the battle, a "tourist camp" sprung up next to Lee's Headquarters. Larson's Cottages featured seven cabins at a rate of $1 to $4 a night. "General Robert E. Lee and his staff planned one of America's greatest battles at this site," says a roadside marker. "Almost a century later the site began offering overnight accommodations to travelers coming to pay homage to their heroes." (achs)

An occupant, 53-year-old Emma Feister, was cited "with keeping a bawdy house and place for the practice of fornication to the common nuisance and disturbance of the neighborhood."

"The talk about the house has been such that battlefield guides have not pointed it out because of explanations that might be made necessary if a visit to Lee's Headquarters was suggested," the local newspaper wagged. "It is to be hoped that this historical landmark can be so restored as to be pointed to and visited by those interested in the battlefield."

But alas, the War Department passed over the building as it acquired land for what would become Gettysburg National Military Park. Instead, the house remained in private ownership, and in 1921, was formally converted into "General Lee's Headquarters Museum." In more recent times, a national hotel franchise occupied the grounds and rented out the top room of the museum to hotel guests.

Calling Lee's Head-quarters "one of America's most significant unprotected sites," the Civil War Trust launched a national fund-raising campaign in 2014 to buy the house and the surrounding four acres. Because the property rests outside the Congressionally authorized boundary of the military park, the Trust worked out an agreement with the nonprofit Gettysburg Foundation to serve as stewards for the house.

Across the road from Lee's Headquarters, the Lutheran Theological Seminary still tops Seminary Ridge. According to its website, the Gettysburg Seminary "Gettysburg Seminary is the oldest of the eight seminaries of the Evangelical Lutheran Church in America (ELCA), tracing its start to 1826 by Samuel Simon Schmucker."

In the years after the Civil War, veterans and the public alike gathered to observe the anniversary of major battles. To help support the influx of visitors for the 75th anniversary of the battle of Gettysburg, the Larson family, owners of the property near Lee's Headquarters, constructed rental cottages that offered all the comforts of home for weary travelers. This lone remaining gas pump that serviced these cottages serves as a link to battlefield trampers who came before us. It's decorated with a portrait of Lt. Col. Rufus Dawes of the 6th Wisconsin, whose men fought along the nearby unfinished railroad cut. (cm)

In July 2014, the Civil War Trust announced plans to acquire and preserve Lee's Headquarters. At the announcement, Licensed Battlefield Guide Timothy H. Smith offered dignitaries a special program on the property's history. (cwt)

Prior to the sesquicentennial of the battle of Gettysburg, the Gettysburg Seminary, the Adams County Historical Society, and the Seminary Ridge Historic Preservation Foundation teamed up to create the Gettysburg Seminary Ridge Museum, which opened on the 150th anniversary of the battle. A hospital wagon sits outside, and banners along Seminary Ridge (on the opposite side of the building) mark the museum well. Today, visitors can make their way to the top of the same building that John Buford observed the battle from. Hours vary. www.seminaryridgemuseum.org. (cm)

In 1832, Reverend Schmucker oversaw the construction of the cupola-topped building that remains probably one of the most recognizable landmarks on the battlefield (and which, today, bears his name as Shmucker Hall). In 1973, the building was placed on the National Register of Historic Places.

OPPOSITE: A statue of Martin Luther was installed next to the chapel of the Lutheran Seminary in 1947. An inscription on its base reads: "Truth is Mightier than Eloquence, The Spirit Stronger than Genius, Faith Greater than Learning." (cm)

Where Was Jeb Stuart?

APPENDIX A
BY ERIC J. WITTENBERG

For want of a nail the shoe was lost,
For want of a shoe the horse was lost;
And for want of a horse the rider was lost;
Being overtaken and slain by the enemy,
All for want of care about a horse-shoe nail.

— Benjamin Franklin (1758)

On June 22, 1863, Maj. Gen. J.E.B. Stuart, the commander of the Army of Northern Virginia's Cavalry division, received orders from Gen. Robert E. Lee to take five brigades of cavalry and Capt. James Breathed's battery of horse artillery on an expedition. Stuart's troopers were to gather supplies for the use of the army and do all the damage they could to Meade's army along the way.

As a result of his maneuvers, though, Stuart would get cut off from the army, and what was supposed to be a three- or four-day excursion lasted far longer than intended, depriving Lee of his eyes and ears at a time when he needed them the most.

Stuart and his troopers were to depart from Rector's Crossroads in the Loudoun Valley of northern Virginia. If Stuart found that the Army of the Potomac was moving north, and if he felt that two brigades of cavalry commanded by Brig. Gen. Beverly H. Robertson and Brig. Gen. William E. "Grumble" Jones could safely cover the various mountain passes through South Mountain and the Bull Run Mountains, then Stuart was to cross the Potomac River east of South Mountain, move through Maryland, and search for Lt. Gen. Richard S. Ewell's troops, who would be operating in Pennsylvania

The Cumberland County Courthouse in Carlisle, Pennsylvania, still bears the marks of Stuart's visit. Damage on the second pillar from the left is identified by white lettering: "July 1, 1863." (mw)

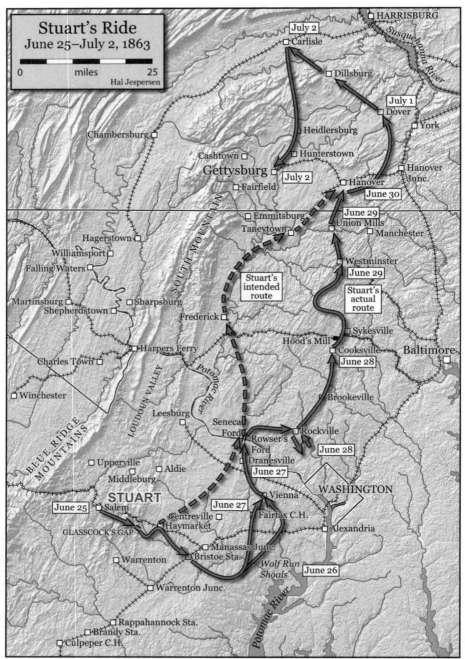

STUART'S RIDE—Lee gave Stuart explicit orders and expected his cavalryman to be gone only three or four days at most, but Stuart ended up being gone for eight. The expedition was behind schedule from the minute it reached Glasscock's Gap, and Stuart further delayed it by waiting for ten hours at Buckland Mills to meet up with Confederate raider John S. Mosby, who was unable to rendezvous or get word to Stuart. Meanwhile, the Union army began shifting northward, continually blocking Stuart's routes to reunite with Lee and throwing Stuart well off course.

somewhere between York and Harrisburg. The orders were quite specific with respect to where Stuart should cross the Potomac and what he was supposed to do.

Relying upon intelligence gathered by Maj. John S. Mosby, who had been Stuart's favorite scout before being given command of an independent force of guerrillas, Stuart and his command marched on June 24. Mosby reported that the way through Glasscock's Gap through the Bull Run Mountains was open. However, when Stuart and his column arrived at the mouth of the gap, they found the Army of the Potomac's II Corps arrayed in the valley below, making its way toward the Potomac River. Stuart had Breathed unlimber his guns and toss a few shells, and a brief skirmish occurred. However, Stuart, recognizing his 4000 cavalry and four guns were insufficient to tangle with the Army of the Potomac's best infantry, broke off, withdrew, and went to Buckland Mills to wait for Mosby.

Jeb Stuart expected a dashing jaunt around the Union army similar to his famous exploit on the Virginia Peninsula in the spring of 1862. This time, things turned out less jaunty. (loc)

Ten hours later, when Mosby had not arrived, Stuart moved out. He swung south to go around the II Corps, crossed Bull Run at Wolf Run Shoals, and then headed for Fairfax Court House, which had been the headquarters of the Army of the Potomac. As they approached Fairfax Station on the Orange & Alexandria Railroad, a force of about 100 Union cavalrymen unexpectedly charged the head of Stuart's column. After a brief melee and after allowing his troopers an opportunity to enjoy the bounty of supplies left behind by the Army of the Potomac, Stuart moved out again, headed for the Potomac River.

Arriving at Rowser's Ford, the only unguarded crossing along the river, Stuart's men took several hours to make their way across the Potomac. They then captured a detachment of Union engineer officers, and moved out on the morning of June 28. As they advanced on Rockville, Maryland, the grayclad troopers spotted a column of 150 brand new Union supply wagons loaded with high-grade fodder. Stuart captured the wagon train, which stirred havoc in Washington, D.C., but which also slowed his column's advance. What would normally have been a great bounty now served as a detriment.

Today, historical markers like this one in Dillsburg, Pennsylvania, are scattered like breadcrumbs along Stuart's route. (cm)

The Confederates then moved on to Sykesville, Maryland, where they captured a detachment of Maryland infantrymen at a railroad depot, destroyed the telegraph lines, and then moved—narrowly missing the chance to capture Maj. Gen. Joseph Hooker, who had just been relieved of command of the Army of the Potomac and was headed to Washington, D.C.

Stuart then headed for Westminster, Maryland, where a detachment of about 90 troopers of the 1st Delaware Cavalry unexpectedly charged them. Nearly all of the Federals were captured, but two officers of the 4th Virginia Cavalry were killed. This brave but foolhardy charge by the

The Picket Memorial in downtown Hanover, Pennsylvania, honors the horsemen of Brig. Gen. Judson Kilpatrick's command, who engaged Stuart's men in battle on June 30, 1863. The bronze statue was dedicated by the Commonwealth on Sept. 28, 1905. The dog, "Mr. Mike," is actually a stand alone sculpture; originally, The Picket was flanked by a pair of cannon. (cm)

First State men cost Stuart several hours. He then marched to Union Mills, near the Mason-Dixon Line, where his command camped for the night of June 29-30.

Moving out early on the morning of June 30, Stuart's troopers encountered Union cavalry commanded by Brig. Gen. Judson Kilpatrick near Hanover, Pennsylvania, and a full day of hard combat occurred in the streets of the town and in the surrounding farm fields. Stuart himself was nearly captured, narrowly escaping from pursuing New York cavalrymen. Late in the day, Kilpatrick broke off and withdrew, and Stuart let him do so. Stuart and his column then made a grueling night march from Hanover to York, where the cavalier expected to find Maj. Gen. Jubal A. Early's infantry division. However, Early had moved out on the morning of June 30 after receiving orders for the Army of Northern Virginia to concentrate at Cashtown, a few miles west of Gettysburg. Early had heard the

Stuart lept this ditch, which was wider and deepr at the time, to escape capture during the battle of Hanover. (cm)

guns at Hanover, but had just moved on instead of investigating, meaning that the opportunity to rendezvous with Stuart's cavalry was lost.

Unsure what to do next, but believing Ewell's other two divisions were operating between the Pennsylvania state capital at Harrisburg and Carlisle, Stuart decided to head for Carlisle, an important town on the Valley Turnpike in the Cumberland Valley. Stuart left the brigade of Wade Hampton and the captured wagon train at Dillsburg and then headed to Carlisle with the brigades of Fitzhugh Lee and John R. Chambliss, Jr. and Breathed's guns.

Another of Stuart's calling cards on the courthouse in Carlisle. (mw)

Arriving at Carlisle about 6:00 p.m. on July 1, Stuart was surprised to find not Ewell's infantry awaiting him, but a division of Union infantry from the defenses of Harrisburg. Stuart unlimbered Breathed's guns, which spent the evening shelling the town of Carlisle after the Union commander refused to surrender. The Confederate cavalrymen set the town gas works ablaze and also burned the Carlisle Barracks, an important U.S. Army installation.

That day, Stuart had sent staff officers out in an attempt to find the Army of Northern Virginia. One, Maj. Andrew R. Venable, heard the guns at Gettysburg and rode to them. He found Ewell, who took him to Robert E. Lee. Lee ordered Venable to tell Stuart that the army was concentrating at Gettysburg.

Venable reached Carlisle well after midnight on the morning of July 2, and relayed Lee's orders to Stuart. The Confederate horse soldiers moved out about 3:00 a.m, Stuart finally arrived at Gettysburg about 2:00 p.m. on July 2 after a long night of difficult marching over South Mountain.

His ride was over.

Stuart had left detailed instructions for Beverly Robertson to follow along behind the Army of Northern Virginia with his brigade and that of Jones. Had Robertson obeyed those orders, those two brigades of cavalry would have reached Chambersburg in plenty of time to escort Lee's column east toward its date with destiny at Gettysburg. However, Robertson disobeyed those orders, dawdled, and did not arrived in Pennsylvania until the morning of July 3. Robertson's failure meant that Hill's Third Corps marched toward its meeting with John Buford's troopers along the Chambersburg Pike without the benefit of a cavalry screen.

For the want of a nail, a kingdom was lost.

ERIC J. WITTENBERG *is an award-winning Civil War historian who focuses on cavalry actions. He is the author of 18 books on the Civil War, including* Plenty of Blame to Go Around: Jeb Stuart's Controversial Ride to Gettysburg *(co-authored with J. David Petruzzi). Eric is a practicing attorney in Columbus, Ohio, and a contributor to* Emerging Civil War.

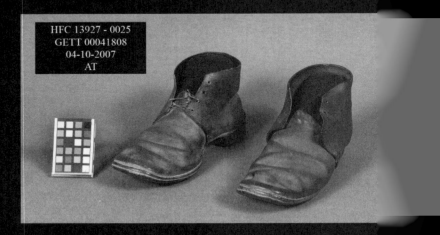

HFC.13927 - 0025
GETT 00041808
04-10-2007
AT

Federal shoes are in
Gettysburg now—but there's
little evidence of a big stash
there in 1863. (gnmp)

Shoes or No Shoes!

APPENDIX B
BY MATT ATKINSON

"Fresh Reinforcements" read the advertisement in *The Adams Centinel*. "Our stock of BOOTS, SHOES, GAITERS, &c., was never more complete." In the years since, no other battle in history has possibly had more controversy surrounding such a small item—footwear—and the accidental meeting of the two armies at Gettysburg.

Gettysburg contained approximately 2,400 residents in 1863. The town was up and coming, the meeting point of ten roads, a center of commerce for Adams County. Farmers sold their produce and spent their proceeds on goods in towns—and maybe on even a drink or two. Hotels sprang up, taverns stayed open late, and various stores began to stock all kinds of goods. The majority of the population worked as artisans and among them were twenty-two people making shoes and boots. Daily life went on; the war had not directly touched the peaceful town—yet.

Robert E. Lee and his Confederate army marched, or in some cases limped, north in search of victory. They were also in search of supplies. "A halt at Williamsport was absolutely necessary from the condition of the feet of the unshod men," Maj. Gen. Robert Rodes noted. "Very many of these gallant fellows were still marching in ranks, with feet bruised, bleeding, and swollen. . . . None but the best of soldiers could have made such a march under such circumstances."

Randolph Shotwell blamed the quartermaster department for the deficiency, stating "it is a well known fact, and a most disgraceful one, that when General Lee crossed the Potomac fully ten thousand of his men were barefooted, blanketless, and hatless! The roads were lined with stragglers limping on swollen and blistered feet. . . !"

John Dooley had the unenviable task of sweeping these stragglers along. He candidly admitted that many soldiers "may have thrown away their shoes purposely so as to have an excuse for desertion and straggling, still their feet [were] bruised and even bleeding, and it is a hard thing to keep these men upon the move."

The exact number of shoeless Confederates will never be known but the figure had to reach thousands, if not tens of thousands. Lee's soldiers needed shoes.

* * *

Gettysburg's citizens received a rude introduction to war on June 26 with the arrival of Jubal Early's division. "Most of the men were exceedingly dirty, some ragged, some without shoes, and some surmounted by the skeleton of what was once an entire hat, affording unmistakable evidence that they stood in great need of having their scanty wardrobe replenished," recalled Professor Michael Jacobs, "and hence the eagerness with which they inquired after shoes, hat and clothing stores, and their disappointment when they were informed that goods of that description were not to be had in town."

Sarah Broadhead echoed these sentiments, remembering the Confederates as "a miserable-looking set. They wore all kinds of hats and caps, even to heavy fur ones, and some were barefooted."

Despite his earnest demands, Early succeeded "in securing only a very small quantity of commissary supplies" and marched his division on to York.

Lee's objective was Harrisburg, the capital of Pennsylvania. All that changed on June 28 with the arrival of a scout named Harrison. He informed Lee that the Union army had crossed the Potomac River and had begun to move west to threaten the Confederate line of communication. Consequently, Lee ordered his far-flung units to assemble to the east of the South Mountain range to prevent this from occurring. The Gettysburg region became the area of concentration. Lee also admonished his subordinates not to bring on a general engagement until the army had concentrated.

Ambrose P. Hill's corps led the advance from the west with the division of Henry Heth in the vanguard. On the night of June 29, Heth's men encamped at Cashtown, nine miles to the west of Gettysburg. The next day Heth sent James Pettigrew's brigade marching down the Chambersburg Pike with orders to "search the town for army supplies (shoes especially), and return the same day."

Heth's statement is important because some Gettysburg buffs accuse Heth of inventing this story in the post-war years. However, the first mention of "shoes" is written in his after-action report of September 3, 1863.

Captain Louis G. Young, Pettigrew's adjutant, recalled preemptory orders not to bring on a fight. Heth advised Pettigrew that a contingent of home guard might be present but if "he should find any organized troops capable of making resistance, or any portion of the Army of the Potomac, he should not attack it."

The next day, June 30, Pettigrew marched his command to town. Along the way, "Longstreet's spy" and a member of the Knights of the Golden Circle informed Pettigrew that John Buford's Union cavalry division lay ahead. Upon reaching the outskirts, Pettigrew observed Union forces to the south and dutifully sent a message back to Heth of his findings and asked for guidance. Heth responded with disbelief that regular Union forces were in Gettysburg but reiterated his former instructions not to bring on a general engagement. Therefore, Pettigrew decided to pull back to Cashtown.

Upon arriving, Pettigrew was making his report to Heth when A.P. Hill rode up. Heth had Pettigrew repeat his story to the corps commander. Heth later wrote that both he and Hill were incredulous that Union forces were in Gettysburg. "Hill said, as I had done," Heth wrote later, "that there was any force at Gettysburg except possibly a small cavalry vidette."

Captain Young stated that "they expressed their doubts so positively" that Pettigrew asked him to join the conversation. Since Young had previously served under Hill, Pettigrew hoped his report would carry "some weight."

Young expressed the opinion that the soldiers that had followed their return to Cashtown were not home guard but regular troops. Hill again expressed doubt "and in emphatic words, expressed the hope that it was, as this was the place he wanted it to be." Young believed that this "spirit of disbelief" had so affected the top officers that no one but Pettigrew believed they were marching into a confrontation.

With that, Heth turned to Hill and said, "If there is no objection, I will march my division tomorrow, go to Gettysburg and secure those shoes."

"Do so," Hill replied.

Heth and Hill may not have believed that Union forces were in Gettysburg, but they certainly knew how to hedge their bets. Hill ordered not one brigade forward, not one division forward, but two divisions backed by two battalions of artillery. In Civil War parlance, that was enough firepower to pick a fight with about any size Union contingent encountered. The rest is history.

In conclusion, there are two main points concerning the connection of shoes and the battle of Gettysburg.

First, Hill, Heth, and even Pettigrew, were unaware that Early had already cleaned out Gettysburg of supplies on June 26. Heth told Pettigrew that Early had successfully requisitioned supplies from Carlisle, Chambersburg, and Shippensburg. "It was supposed that it would be the same at Gettysburg," Young noted. In other words, "perception is reality." We know today there were not any supplies in Gettysburg, but Heth truly believed it.

Second, Hill and Heth disobeyed Lee's directive to not bring on a general engagement. The two generals personified the type of officer Lee wanted in the Army of Northern Virginia: independent, aggressive, and confident. In this instance, however, there was nothing to be gained by marching to Gettysburg—not even shoes. Perhaps this confidence, this belief in themselves and their men, overcame their better judgment.

Perhaps the question we should ask today is: who surprised Robert E. Lee at Gettysburg—the Yankees or A. P. Hill?

MATT ATKINSON *is a ranger/ historian with Gettysburg National Military Park.*

The Most Second-Guessed Decision of the War

APPENDIX C
BY CHRIS MACKOWSKI
AND KRISTOPHER D. WHITE

It's arguably the most second-guessed decision of the Civil War: On the first day of the battle of Gettysburg, after a bruising fight north of town sent the Union army into retreat, Confederate Gen. Robert E. Lee ordered his Second Corps commander, Lt. Gen. Richard Ewell, to attack the new Federal position on Cemetery Hill "if practicable."

Ewell chose not to attack, allowing the Union army to reform on the hill and dig in, and that position then served as the lynchpin for the entire Federal line. Ever since, armchair generals have said, "If Stonewall Jackson had been there instead of Ewell. . . ." The implication, of course, is that the legendary Jackson would've found it "practicable" to attack and would have, naturally, swept the Union army from the field.

But Ewell, who had taken command after Jackson had died a month and a half earlier, had several good reasons for not attacking the Union position—reasons frequently ignored or overlooked because of post-war scapegoating. As a result, modern students of the battle get only part of the story. They see Ewell as a man who failed to live up to his predecessor's glory rather than as a newly minted corps commander who made a sound military decision.

* * *

Thomas Jonathan "Stonewall" Jackson looms large in the story of Ewell at Gettysburg because Jackson's career as Ewell's predecessor shapes the way people have looked at Ewell's performance. Jackson earned a reputation for aggressiveness and independence, frequently serving as Lee's hammer. If ordered to do something, Jackson did it—in his cut-and-dried approach to military discipline, an order was an order and had to be obeyed.

It's a small leap, then, to assume that if Jackson had been ordered to take Cemetery Hill "if practicable," his aggressive nature would have found it practicable. He would have found a way to obey the order. "Oh, for the presence and inspiration of Old Jack for just one hour!" lamented Jackson's former chief of staff, Maj. Alexander "Sandie" Pendleton, who went on to serve under Ewell.

There are two major flaws behind that assumption, however.

"It is a fact not generally known . . . that in all his famous flank movements Gen. Jackson was careful

To believe his critics, Richard Ewell's major mistake on July 1 seems to be that he wasn't Stonewall Jackson. (cm)

to examine the ground to learn the exact position of the enemy," wrote Southern war correspondent Peter Wellington Alexander for the *Charleston Mercury*, "and hence his blows were always well aimed and terrible in effect."

Jackson learned a hard lesson at Kernstown in March of 1862, when faulty intelligence about the enemy's position led to his only battlefield defeat. Ever after, Jackson made a concerted effort to gather information about his opponent's dispositions. In fact, it was in the midst of one such attempt at gathering information that Jackson had been accidentally shot by his own men during the battle of Chancellorsville.

To assume that Jackson would've stormed Cemetery Hill without having any idea of what lay beyond it places too much emphasis on Jackson's aggressiveness at the expense of his good sense as a tactician.

The second problem that underpins assumptions about Jackson lies in the wording of Lee's orders. Over the years, much attention has been given to Lee's particular wording: "General Ewell was, therefore, instructed to carry the hill occupied by the enemy, if he found it practicable. . . ."

As outlined in Chapter Twelve, Ewell had plenty of legitimate reasons to think an assault on Cemetery Hill wasn't practicable: his men were disorganized and tired, he had no hope of support from the rest of the army, and he had credible reports of a threat on his left flank.

It's most important to note, though, that the words "if practicable" never appear in print until Lee filed his revised report of the battle in January of 1864, more than six months afterward. The words never appear anywhere in print before then.

Certainly, though, the intent behind Lee's orders on the afternoon of July 1, 1863, seems unmistakable. He urged Ewell to attack if his corps commander thought it advantageous to do so. But Lee also placed a very important qualification on his order—a qualification best understood by looking at the complete passage from Lee's report:

> *Without information as to its proximity, the strong position which the enemy had assumed could not be attacked without danger of exposing the four divisions present, already weakened and exhausted by a long and bloody struggle, to overwhelming numbers of fresh troops. General Ewell was, therefore, instructed to carry the hill occupied by the enemy, if he found it practicable, but to avoid a general engagement until the arrival of the other divisions of the army, which were to hasten forward.*

Unfortunately, in the years since the battle, much emphasis has been placed on the phrase "if practicable"—

specific words that Lee may have never uttered on July 1, 1863—and the warning about avoiding a general engagement has been ignored altogether.

* * *

Major General Isaac Trimble, attached on special duty to Ewell's command during the battle, was among those who tried to dismiss Lee's warning. Writing for the Southern Historical Society (SHS) years after Lee and Ewell had both died, Trimble recalls his attempt to persuade Ewell to attack. As Trimble remembers it, Ewell called attention to Lee's order not to bring on a general engagement. "[T]hat hardly applies to things," Trimble responded, "as we have fought a hard battle already, and should secure the advantage gained."

In Trimble's version of the story, he urged Ewell to take not Cemetery Hill, where the Union army was trying to reform, but nearby Culp's Hill. "General, *there* is an eminence of commanding position, and not now occupied, as it ought to be by us or the enemy soon. I advise you to send a brigade and hold it if we are to remain here," Trimble said, adding that "it ought to be held by us at once."

"When I need advice from a junior officer, I generally ask it," Ewell replied.

Trimble never forgot the insult. In his report to the SHS, he made an effort to paint Ewell as being "far from composure" and "under much embarrassment" and said Ewell "moved about uneasily, a good deal excited" and "undecided what to do next."

"[F]ailure to follow up vigorously on our success . . . was the first fatal error committed," Trimble wrote. "It seemed to me that General Ewell was in a position to do so. But he evidently did not feel that he should take so responsible a step without orders from General Lee. . . ."

Michael Shaara's novel *The Killer Angels* dramatically retells the story of Trimble's encounter with Ewell. The scene translates well in the film version of *Gettysburg* thanks to the compelling performance by William Morgan Sheppard, who plays Trimble. Nowhere in the book or film does Ewell get to tell his side of the story, though, so modern audiences typically accept Trimble's version as truth.

Jubal Early, too, had a vested interest in blaming Ewell for the lack of action on the late afternoon and evening of July 1. Ewell had ordered Early to take Culp's

Crusty Maj. Gen. Isaac Trimble found the perfect platform for his Ewell bashing nearly ninety years after his death: Michael Shaara's Pulitzer Prize-winning novel *The Killer Angels*, which depicts Trimbles side of the story with great dramatic effect but without exploring Ewell's perspective. In the movie version, *Gettysburg*, the scene is one of the film's most memorable. (loc, cm)

With the foliage down, the town is in ready view from Benner's Hill. Elements of the XII Corps had been moving around this area, giving Richard Ewell good reason to pause before making any aggressive pursuit of the retreating XI Corps. Had Federals occupied the hill, which sat on Ewell's left flank, it would have turned Confederates into easy targets as they swept through the town in their assault. (cm)

Hill, which was unoccupied and which would have made the Federal position on Cemetery Hill untenable. Although Early's division had sustained only 500 casualties in the afternoon's fight—compared to about 2,500 in Rodes' division—Early claimed his men couldn't take it. Ewell asked Edward "Allegheny" Johnson's men to move against it instead, but by the time Johnson got into position, Federals had realized their vulnerability and had taken the ground for themselves.

Early's refusal turned out to have catastrophic consequences for the Army of Northern Virginia. Over the next two days, assaults on Culp's Hill would lead to some 2,500 Confederate casualties during the longest-sustained combat on the Gettysburg battlefield.

After the war, Early contended that he had vigorously supported an assault on Cemetery Hill, yet on the very evening of the battle, he claimed his men were too worn out and disorganized to occupy the unoccupied Culp's Hill. If his men were in no condition to move unopposed to an empty hilltop, how could they have led an attack against a heavily fortified enemy position?

"The discovery that this lost us the battle," wrote Campbell Brown, "is one of those frequently-recurring but tardy strokes of military genius of which one hears long after the minute circumstances that rendered them at the time impracticable, are forgotten—at least I heard nothing of it for months & months, & it was several years before any claim was put in by Early or his friends that his advice had been in favor of an attack & had been neglected."

In fact, Early led a vigorous campaign—after Lee's death, so that Lee could not refute any of Early's claims—to place the blame for the loss at Gettysburg on Ewell. Early also cast vitriol at First Corps commander James Longstreet for actions on July 2 and 3. Trimble, cavalryman Fitzhugh Lee, and others readily joined in. That scapegoating has since become accepted as a central tenet to Lost Cause mythology.

"It was a moment of most critical importance, more critical to us now, than it would seem to anyone then," staff officer Capt. James Power Smith wrote after the war, enjoying the benefit of hindsight. "Our corps commander, General Ewell, as true a Confederate soldier as ever went into battle, was simply waiting for orders, when every moment of the time could not be balanced with gold."

But tactically Ewell did the right thing on the evening of July 1. His ultimate decision not to assault Cemetery Hill was a sound military judgment based on the evidence he had at the time weighed against the discretionary orders that came from his commander. Critics have second-guessed Ewell's judgment about the "practicability" of an assault, ignoring the fact that Lee expressly forbade him from bringing on a general engagement.

In the years since, a well-coordinated finger-pointing campaign, a suppression of facts, and a nation's admiration for a martyred Confederate icon all combined to vilify Ewell and his well-reasoned decision under pressure.

An extended version of this article appeared as the cover story of the August 2010 issue of Civil War Times.

The John Reynolds equestri-
statue along the Chambersbu
Pike overlooks the area whe
Reynolds fell. (

Reynolds Reconsidered
APPENDIX D
BY KRISTOPHER D. WHITE

The question that has always lingered in my mind: Was John Reynolds a great corps commander?

Major General John Fulton Reynolds' reputation as corps commander has always baffled me as an historian. His only real test at that level came at Fredericksburg. Prior to that battle, Reynolds' Civil War fighting record was solid, but nothing one would call stellar.

Reynolds, who came from a fairly well-connected family, was a West Point graduate of the class of 1841. He served in the artillery and was brevetted twice for bravery in the Mexican-American War. In the pre-war army, he was well-connected with many of the names we know so well from the Civil War, so when the war broke out, he knew many of the right people.

He began his Civil War career with the 14th United States Infantry, then moved over to brigade command in the Pennsylvania Reserve Division. In the spring of 1862, he was appointed the military governor of Fredericksburg, Virginia. Other than a few skirmishes in the area, he had little to do, although he did garner a great deal of good will among the civilian population of the small southern city.

On the Peninsula, in 1862, Reynolds fought his brigade at Beaver Dam Station, but was captured at Gaines' Mill while asleep. Confederate Major General Daniel Harvey Hill, whose men captured the general, told Reynolds, "he ought not to fret at the fortunes of war, which were notoriously fickle." Although Reynolds attempted to write the embarrassment off in letters home, I often wonder how a general with at least a handful of staff officers gets left behind on the field—asleep.

Following his exchange, Reynolds took command of the Pennsylvania Reserves Division. He showed great personal bravery at Second Manassas, and his division absorbed much of the Confederate onslaught on August 30. As the Southern steamroller took aim at Henry House Hill, Col. Henry Benning's brigade exposed their flank to one of Reynolds' brigades. Leading by example, Reynolds—on foot— seized the flag of the 2nd Pennsylvania Reserves and led the balance of Brig. Gen. George G. Meade's brigade into the Georgians' flank. This was a great act of bravery, but he took himself from a division commander to essentially a regimental commander by his actions.

Photographer Matthew Brady
(right) and an assistant visited
Gettysburg just days after the
battle. Standing in the field
behind McPherson's barn, the
assistant points toward Herbst
Woods and the area where
Reynolds was shot. (loc)

Post-Second Manassas, Reynolds went to Pennsylvania to command the state troops during the Antietam Campaign. When he returned to the Army of the Potomac, he assumed command of I Corps.

At Fredericksburg, on December 13, men of Reynolds' corps broke through at Prospect Hill. This was the only Federal breakthrough at Fredericksburg. In reality, Reynolds had little to do with the breakthrough itself. Rather, he actually had more to do with hindering the short-lived gains. When both Meade (now a major general) and Brig. Gen. John Gibbon's divisions broke the Southern lines at Fredericksburg, they could not receive timely reinforcements. Their corps commander could not be found. Meade sent a number of messengers to Reynolds begging for reinforcements, but none could locate him.

That's because the corps commander was on the Federal artillery line, personally ordering batteries where to fire, how to elevate, and at times—according to some accounts—was off his horse sighting guns himself. This was not the job of a major general—it was the job of Col. Charles Wainwright, the capable I Corps chief of artillery. In reality, Reynolds demoted himself from a corps commander to a battalion commander, and did so at a time his subordinates needed him the most.

"A close search of the records reveals that Reynolds spent most of his time worrying the artillery about ephemeral details rather than monitoring the overall situation," says Fredericksburg historian Francis A. O'Reilly, who goes on to say, "At one time or another, every battery in the First Corps encountered, received advice from, or took orders from Reynolds . . . [which]

The Reynolds equestrian statue weighs four and a half tons. Sculptor Henry Kirke Bush-Brown also did the equestrian statues of Meade and Sedgwick, and he sculpted the bust of Lincoln that serves as the centerpiece of the Lincoln Speech Memorial in the national cemetery. (loc)

made him completely ineffective when Meade sought critical reinforcements."

The following spring, during the Chancellorsville Campaign, the I Corps did very little fighting. In fact, of the 16,908 men that Reynolds fielded during the campaign, only 300 were listed among the casualty rolls at the end of battle. During the riverine crossing at Second Fredericksburg, Brig. Gen. Wadsworth led part of the famed Iron Brigade across the river and forced a landing, which was a much heavier task than it should have been since Reynolds did little to coordinate his efforts with another crossing force up the Rappahannock River. Following the crossing, I Corps was called from Fredericksburg to Chancellorsville, but they were held in the rear of the army for much of the battle. On the night of May 4, during a council of war among the Federal high command, which was to decide if the army was to stay and fight it out or retreat, Reynolds fell asleep—again.

"[A]s a commander . . . [Renynolds] rarely acted the rank that he held." (loc)

Then, of course, there was Gettysburg. While acting as a wing commander, where he oversaw fully one-third of Meade's cavalry and nearly one-half of Meade's infantry, Reynolds was killed. At the time of his death, Reynolds was actually acting, at best, like a brigade commander and, at worst, a regimental commander as he moved forward with the 2nd Wisconsin Infantry.

The great issue I have with Reynolds as a commander is that he rarely acted the rank that he held. At Fredericksburg, he was not where he was needed— in the rear, in an easy-to-find place for his subordinates. There, he should have been assisting with reinforcements and driving Stonewall Jackson from the field.

Former officers and enlisted men of the I Corps raised $15,000 to install a statue of John Reynolds in the national cemetery. Oddly, officers were allowed to donate no more than $5.00 to the monument, while enlisted men could donate no more than $.50. (cm)

At Gettysburg, he was a wing commander, and he should have been nowhere near the main battle line. The closest spot to action he should have been would have been the Lutheran Theological Seminary. Even the vapid Oliver Otis Howard, when he assumed Reynolds' role, knew that he needed to be in an easily recognizable place, nowhere near the front lines, where he could be readily found by the men. (That is not to say that Howard did not make mistakes of his own).

On top of all of this, Reynolds did not choose the ground on which to fight at Gettysburg. John Buford did. Yet today, Reynolds' role greatly overshadows those of Buford, William Gamble, Abner Doubleday, and a slew of others.

After his death, Reynolds was treated as a hero. Much of this was not because of Reynolds' actions, but the actions of his staff and others. Reynolds' death itself came in the heat of battle at the height of a major Union crisis, where he was felled on home soil. Some of the accounts written by his staff were not so much written to glorify Reynolds, but written to garner favor from Reynolds' family and friends, since one of his staff officers was brought up on rape charges.

Alfred Waud produced a famous sketch of his death, drawing wide attention to the incident. Then of course there are the slew of monuments erected by the survivors of the corps and others, including three monuments on the field to Reynolds himself and another statue that's part of the Pennsylvania state monument.

As a leader of men, there is no doubt Reynolds was brave to a fault. The problem with his bravery was that it took Reynolds from a Division, Corps, and Wing commander down to a regimental commander at the greatest moment of crisis—a tendency he repeated time and again.

One has to ask: Was Maj. Gen. John F. Reynolds really a great corps commander, or was he just killed at the right place at the right time?

KRISTOPHER D. WHITE *is co-founder of Emerging Civil War. White is a former Licensed Battlefield Guide at Gettysburg and a former historian for the National Park Service.*

Alfred Waud did several rough sketches of his "Death of Reynolds" (above) before settling on a design that became a final print (bottom). (loc)

For years, historians believed
the "Harvest of Death"—
one of the most iconic photos
of Gettysburg—was located
on the July 2 battlefield,
but recent research suggests
it was taken on the July 1
battlefield. (loc)

The Harvest of Death

APPENDIX E

BY JAMES BROOKES

Slowly, over the misty fields of Gettysburg—as all reluctant to expose their ghastly horrors to the light—came the sunless morn, after the retreat by Lee's broken army. Through the shadowy vapors, it was, indeed, a "harvest of death" that was presented; hundreds and thousands of torn Union and rebel soldiers—although many of the former were already interred—strewed the now quiet fighting ground, soaked by the rain, which for two days had drenched the country with its fitful showers.

So Alexander Gardner began his description of the photographer Timothy H. O'Sullivan's "A Harvest of Death." The photograph presents the human wreckage of the battle of Gettysburg following that momentous three-day engagement. Gardner calls his readers to envisage the grotesque scene of death revealing itself from the mist. The image stands as the most prominent of a series of images of the slain of Gettysburg. Reflecting briefly on the torrential rain that had saturated the earth following the battle, Gardner suggests that the very landscape has mourned over the men who have been rendered a "harvest of death" with their "ghastly horrors."

The photograph, credited to O'Sullivan, was taken when Alexander Gardner led a photographic team through the devastated landscape to document the aftermath of the battle. By noon on July 5, Gardner and his team apparently reached Gettysburg via the Emmitsburg Road and began taking photographs near the Rose Farm.

The Rose Farm area was one of the last to be cleared of the dead, which allowed Gardner's team to find scenes worthy of documentation amongst the burial crews. Whereas other Civil War photographers preferred pastoral landscape views, bustling military camps, and soldiers on parade, due to their greater popularity with the American citizenry, Gardner's team at Gettysburg were very much focused on documenting the casualties of the battle. By 1863, death views were not popular in a nation fatigued by desolation and war, but they stand as essential historical sources for comprehending the terrible realities of Civil War engagements.

In his *Photographic Sketch Book of the War*, Gardner identified the dead in these images as "rebels . . . Killed in the frantic efforts to break the steady lines of an army of patriots." But the soldiers pictured are Federal dead, evident by their uniforms (particularly their blouses and military-issue shirts) and by a stereograph of the same group of dead titled "Federal Soldiers As They Fell, At Battle of Gettysburg" (1863).

It is likely that Gardner retitled the image in 1865 when his *Sketch Book* was published. War-weariness and the omnipresence of death at the end of the conflict made negative images of Union soldiers unpopular in the northern United States, where the audience for Gardner's visual account would be found. Few wanted visual reminders of the death that had consumed so many northern soldiers, so Gardner transformed the deceased into Southerners with his caption. Gardner also omitted all photographs from his 'Dead at Antietam' series from the *Sketch Book*, regardless of their enormous popularity and familiarity at the time of their exhibition. The images of the Gettysburg dead offered viewers an alternative to the anticipated and well-known images from Antietam.

Photographer Timothy O'Sullivan took this photo, "Gettysburg, Pa. Bodies of Federal Soldiers, Killed on July 1, Near the McPherson Woods" as a companion photo to "Harvest of Death." Note a structure that appears to be the Thompson house— known today as "Lee's Headquarters"—in the upper-right corner of the image. (loc)

Though the men were certainly not Confederates, the framing, style, and composition of the photograph differs little from other images of Southern war dead. O'Sullivan's photograph is no celebration of the heroic deeds of a particular Federal regiment, but a mournful recognition of the sacrifices made by the northern soldiery during the conflict.

Despite falsifying the identity of the bodies in O'Sullivan's photograph, Gardner recognized unique details contained within the image. He called the spectator to notice the "shattered bodies" lay "in all conceivable positions," that they lack shoes, have turned-out pockets, and are surrounded by ammunition, rags, canteens, crackers, cups, and other debris littered on the battlefield. O'Sullivan's macabre photograph gives the viewer some conception of the chaos and confusion of battle, even though his subjects lay still and silent.

Colonel Horatio N. Warren of the 142nd Pennsylvania, which carried out their burial work on the July 1 battlefield, remembered the grim duty:

> We found our dead lying where they fell . . . their upturned faces black from the burning rays of the scorching sun . . . it was with much difficulty we were enabled to distinguish one from the other.

The difficulty of identifying bodies is further confirmed by historian Scott Hartwig's statement that, of the thirty-nine men killed in action of the 20th New York State Militia and the 121st Pennsylvania, which both took part in the first day's fighting, only two "lay as unidentified burials in the Soldiers' National Cemetery today."

But Gardner's misrepresentation of the photograph through his postwar caption offers a faint murmur of the controversy that would eventually erupt over the "Harvest of Death" photograph. Feverish debate still occurs over the exact location of this iconic image. Civil War historians and photographic detectives William Frassanito, Garry Adelman, Scott Hartwig, and John Cummings, among others, have all attempted to document where O'Sullivan produced the photographic plate.

In *Gettysburg: A Journey in Time*, Frassanito concluded that the image was taken near the Rose Farm and the Emmitsburg Road. But Hartwig was drawn to the first day's fighting, and eventually concluded that "A Harvest of Death" was taken east of the positions held by Col. Chapman Biddle's brigade on July 1. Frassanito did not find the view because, at the time he wrote his book, a tree screen planted by the National Park Service obscured the historic view. Cummings then provided further evidence that the image was taken on the first day's battlefield. Operating in the same vicinity as Hartwig, he located the image southwest of the Thompson house by matching the horizon in another photograph of the same dead, taken from a different angle, to the present rise on which the house stands. Adelman, who backed the Rose Farm location, made a plea for patience, refuting various other theories about the location of the image and issuing a ten-rule guide for locating Civil War photographs.

Debate also exists over what time and on what date the image was captured and to which regiment the dead soldiers belonged. The latter discussion seems most significant and poignant, for this image has been circulated for more than 150 years among those fascinated by the Civil War, and yet the identity of the soldiers remains unknown. Hartwig urges the present-day spectator to discard their emotional detachment and to contemplate that, though these men are unidentified, on the days that Gardner and O'Sullivan were capturing their photographs, the families of these soldiers waited anxiously for news of their safety. Hartwig directs the viewer to consider what the *New York Times* reporter reviewing the "Dead of Antietam" exhibition in October, 1862 stated the camera could not capture: "the background of widows and orphans, torn from the bosom of their natural protectors." Though the photograph shows only the northern war dead in a destroyed condition, the neglected nature of their bodies calls us to consider those at home— victims, too, who would have comforted them.

"A Harvest of Death" remains a morbid curiosity of Civil War history, enticing historians and the general viewer alike to muse on its depiction and meaning. The controversy surrounding the image's false caption in Gardner's *Sketch Book* only deepens the meaning of its representation, and calls the historian to consider the poignancy of such photographs during and immediately after the conflict. Though the debate over the photograph's location appears to have been concluded, it is likely that others will offer new perspectives on this iconic image.

JAMES BROOKES *is a photographic historian who specializes in the employment of photographic portraiture by Union soldiers. He is a Ph.D. candidate at the University of Nottingham (UK), where he is researching the relationship between visual culture and the rank-and-file soldiery of the American Civil War.*

Near this spot on July 1, 1863 a Union soldier fell mortally wounded. When a local resident found the unidentified body, he also discovered a photograph of three children. News of this poignant find was soon widely covered by the press, and copies of the photograph were distributed and sold for charity. One of these reached Mrs. Philinda Humiston of Portville, New York, who now realized that her husband, Sergeant Amos Humiston of Company C, 154th New York Volunteers, had been killed. The plight of the Humiston children—Frank, Frederick, and Alice—touched an outpouring of sympathy and donations from throughout the North, leading to the establishment of a Soldier's Orphan's Home in Gettysburg in 186_ _____ Humiston's body was removed from here to _____ National Cemetery.

A monument
to Amos Humiston
was dedicated in 1993. (dd)

Amos Humiston and the Children of the Battlefield

APPENDIX F
BY MEG THOMPSON

January 2, 1864, was a cold winter day in western New York, but there was no hint that the train that brought the visitor from Philadelphia was running late. Dr. J. Francis Bourns felt he had finally identified the so-called "children of the battlefield," and he was coming to meet the Humistons. Their tiny home in Portville had been cleaned, and its inhabitants were dressed in freshly pressed clothing. Although these important men had never entered the parlor of Philinda Humiston and her family, they had gathered at the train station to meet Dr. Bourns: the Reverend Isaac Ogden, tall and bearded in a patriarchal manner, and the Reverend John Heyl Vincent, also bearded, but balding. Adam T. Warden, a local blacksmith and a good friend of the little Humiston family, accompanied them. It is recorded that Philinda greeted the men in a "quiet but warm-hearted" manner.

Portville, New York, is south of Buffalo, along the border with Pennsylvania. (cm)

The most eagerly awaited of the visitors was a medium-sized man with long white hair, ferocious white side-whiskers, and piercing blue eyes—Dr. Bourns. Perhaps He looked at Philinda and her children, Fred, Frank, and Alice, in a searching manner and wondered, *Were these three little ones in front of him actually the same children whose images were imprinted on the bloodstained ambrotype?*

After a few minutes of conversation, Dr. Bourns brought the image on glass from his pocket and gently handed it to Philinda. "When the relic . . . was presented to the wife, her hands shook like an aspen leaf," wrote Pastor Ogden, but the saddened wife retained her composure. Then they all, adults and children alike, dropped to their knees and prayed, giving thanks for the Hand of Divine Providence that had guided them to this moment. Unbeknownst to them, Philinda Humiston and her children, nine-year-old Frank, seven-year-old Alice, and five-year-old Fred, were about to become the most famous widow and orphans in the entire Civil War North.

Amos Humiston, a dark-haired fellow of average height who had already spent three years at sea as a whaler, married twenty-three year old Philinda Smith on the 4th of July 1854, in Candor, New York. In 1859, Amos and Philinda, now accompanied

FRANK.   FREDERICK.   ALICE.

"The Children of the Battlefield" captured the public imagination and became one of the nation's great mysteries. (loc)

by two children, moved west to the small township of Portville, in Cattaragus County, New York. Trained in leatherwork, Amos owned the only harness shop in the township, and they were now nearer Philinda's family, which must have been a comfort to a mother of three little children.

Amos's work was regular, and he had enough free time to play with his little family. All accounts say he was a loving and involved family man. Having a family made it easy for Amos to ignore the world beyond the door, but in 1861, the Civil War began. In July 1862, Amos finally left Portville for the armies when President Lincoln made his second call for "300,000 More." The extra money in state bounties helped to reassure him that his wife and children would be provided for. Amos was assigned to the 154th New York.

Amos's regiment became part of the 1st Brigade, 2nd Division, XI Corps, of the Army of the Potomac. Colonel Adolphus Bushbeck of the 27th Pennsylvania commanded their brigade, and they served under Maj. Gen. Franz Sigel. After enduring the miserable winter of 1862-1863 and a change of corps commanders, Amos fought at Chancellorsville and wrote home on a regular basis. He was promoted to sergeant of his small company.

His letters show that he missed his wife and children terribly. "Tel them babies that pa wants to see them very much," he wrote. His words may have urged Philinda to use some of the money he assiduously sent home to have a portrait taken of the children. After it arrived, Amos always carried it with him. In the ambrotype, Baby Fred sits on a chair in the middle, with Alice to his left and Frank to his right. Frank wears a checked shirt made of the same material as the dress worn by Alice, reminding their father that his wife's skill at needlework continued to provide for his *little ones*, as he always referred to the children.

> *May 25, 1863—I would like to be with you to night and the little ones they will forget that they have got a pa but this thing cannot last a great while longer it seames to me I want you to write to me as often as you can and not wait for me and be a good girl and keep your courage up.*

This was the last letter Philinda received from Amos. He was correct: his part in the war was about to end.

That spring, the 11th Corps made long marches through Virginia and into Maryland. On June 28,

Maj. Gen. George Gordon Meade took command of the Army of the Potomac. Meade's Army marched north, following Lee into Pennsylvania and then quickly to Gettysburg. Amos Humiston's unit was initially placed in the vicinity of the Evergreen Cemetery on the morning of July 1. From that vantage point, the terrific din of musketry and cannon signaled a major battle. The men were ordered to move to the north end of the town to reinforce the failing XI Corps line. By the time their brigade reached the edge of town, the corps was broken apart, and Humiston's unit was ordered into Kuhn's Brickyard. The layout of the brickyard provided natural breastworks, but the fighting was fierce, and the unit was forced back with severe losses. By the end of the day, the 265 men of the 154th New York numbered three officers and fifteen men.. Sergeant Amos Humiston was not among those who reported back to his commander.

Instead, Amos lay in a secluded spot on the property of Judge S. R. Russell near the intersection of Stratton and York Streets. History's best guess is that Humiston's body was found after the battle by a young girl who was the daughter of a tavern keeper in nearby Graeffenburg. The dead soldier was still clutching the ambrotype of his children. The girl retrieved the picture and brought it to her father, Benjamin Schriver. Schriver kept the ambrotype on his mantle as an interesting conversation piece.

Sgt. Amos Humiston (above) appears on the Coster Ave. mural (below). Artist Mark Dunkelman painted many of the soldiers' faces from photographs. (md; cm)

Dr. Francis Bourns was a private doctor from Philadelphia who had volunteered as a physician to care for the many wounded soldiers after the battle of Gettysburg. Bourns and four other men were on their way to Gettysburg when their wagon broke down in Graeffenburg. While waiting for repairs, the men heard the story of Gettysburg's dead soldier. They found Schriver so they could see the ambrotype for themselves.

Bourns talked Schriver into giving him the image of the children. He also made sure that the unknown soldier's grave was permanently marked—because Bourns had a plan: perhaps he could use the image in the ambrotype to identify the soldier. If the plan worked, Gettysburg's Unknown Soldier could be disinterred and brought home—wherever that might be.

Through the doctor's network of friends, the ambrotype made its way to Philadelphia. From there it was written about in many Northern newspapers, from *Harper's Weekly* and *Frank Leslie's Illustrated Newspaper* to the tiny *American Presbyterian*, a single copy of which made its way to Portville, New York.

Early in November 1863, Philinda took the October 29 edition of the *AP* into her hands, brought to her by a friend who thought that maybe . . . just maybe.

And, of course, it was. Philinda's friends helped her contact Bourns, who mailed a *carte de visite* copy of the ambrotype to her via express mail. The father of the "children of the battlefield" had been identified, and his widow found as well. All over the North, headlines blared, "The Dead Soldier Identified." The Humistons became famous overnight.

Ulysses S. Grant paid a visit to Gettysburg in the autumn of 1872, stopping at the National Soldiers' Orphans Homestead. (gnmp)

OPPOSITE: The monument to Amos Humiston features his portrait and those of his children. (cm)

The story of "The Children of the Battlefield" was repeated throughout the rest of the nineteenth century and far into the twentieth. A home was set up in Gettysburg for orphans of Civil War soldiers, and Fred, Frank, Alice, and Philinda lived there for several years. When celebrations such as Memorial Day were held to honor the Civil War dead, the story of the ambrotype identification was told again and again. By the 1930s, most of the veterans were dead, and memories of the Civil War dimmed, but during the 1960s Civil War Centennial, both Portville and Gettysburg brought back the oft-told tale, reprinting it in newspapers and magazines nationwide.

On July 3, 1993, a monument was unveiled at the site of Sgt. Amos Humiston's original grave on Judge Russell's property. Of the more than 1,200 monuments that dot the hills, fields, and roadsides of Gettysburg, it is the only one dedicated to an individual enlisted man. It commemorates the love of country and the love of family that prompted so many Northern men to enlist in service and fight the long, terrible fight for union.

MEG THOMPSON, *a regular contributor to Emerging Civil War, is the author of* The Aftermath of Battle: The Burial of the Civil War Dead.

Near this spot on July 1, 1863 a Union soldier
...tally wounded. When a local resident
...entified body, he also discovered a
...children. News of this poig...
...y covered by the pre...
...raph were distributed
...eached Mrs. D...
...ho now

Big Pipe Creek (pg)

Pipe Creek

APPENDIX G
BY RYAN QUINT

Approximately 15-20 miles south and southeast of Gettysburg is Big Pipe Creek, and had everything gone according to George Meade's plan, we would be studying the battle of Pipe Creek rather than the battle of Gettysburg.

By June 30, 1863, Meade had only been in command for three days, and the Army of the Potomac was scattered all over southern Pennsylvania and Maryland. Hoping to collect all his forces and also set up for a defensive battle, Meade had a circular written up on the night of the 13th. "If the enemy assume the offensive, and attack," he wrote, in part, "it is [Meade's] intention . . . to withdraw the army from its present position, and form line of battle with the left resting in the neighborhood of Middleburg, and the right at Manchester, the general direction being that of Pipe Creek."

In other words, if Lee's rebels continued their invasion, Meade's Federals would fall back from the area of Gettysburg and form up along the Pipe Creek.

The two towns that Meade mentioned, Middleburg and Manchester, formed the two anchors for the Federal line. They are about 20 miles from each other as Pipe Creek winds up and down on its way to the Monocacy River. Meade's plan called for the various corps to align themselves on the line within supporting distance of each other, while also blocking the roads to Baltimore and Washington. If Lee wanted to continue, he would be forced to attack Meade's line.

Attracting Meade further to Pipe Creek was Parr's Ridge, an elevation ranging from 800-1,000 feet that stretched behind the creek. As an engineer, George Meade saw the benefit of having a defensive line built atop Parr's Ridge; Federal artillery would be able to sweep the valley in front of them. Meade's opinion was shared by his chief of artillery, Henry Hunt, who voiced after the war that a battle at Pipe Creek would "probably have been better" as opposed to Gettysburg. Hunt went on to say, though, "events finally controlled the actions of both sides."

Hunt's words showcase how battles had a habit of destroying even the most carefully laid plans. And Meade's Pipe Creek Circular *was* a carefully laid plan. Between Middleburg and Manchester, separated by those 20 miles, from left to right would have been the III, I, XI, XII, V, and VI corps. Behind those corps would be the II Corps, held in reserve and ready to deploy to any area threatened by a Confederate assault. It would be a nearly impregnable position; one that would have made the July 3 attack look like a quick afternoon's stroll.

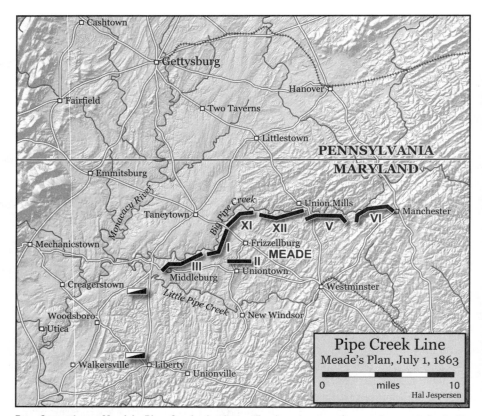

PIPE CREEK LINE—Meade's Pipe Creek circular outlined a plan to seize good ground for battle while protecting the capital to the southeast. While Meade could not be sure of the exact approach Confederates might make, his proposed position would allow him to shift troops over a 20-mile front to concentrate at any point of contact. Civil War Trails signs mark the Pipe Creek Line's left flank at Middleburg, the center at Union Mills, and the right at Uniontown (a community described by the wayside marker as "Patriotic, but paralyzed"). Meade established his headquarters at Taneytown.

The left flank of the Pipe Creek Line in Middleburg, Maryland, looks lonely—a good reflection of Meade's psychological position on the evening of June 30, 1863, when he was new to command and unclear about his enemy's whereabouts. (pg)

But for all that planning, it is likely that the man in charge of the lead elements of the Army of the Potomac, John F. Reynolds, never even got the Pipe Creek Circular. Commanding a wing of the army, Reynolds was the man who would be responsible for pulling his men back to the Pipe Creek Line, and thus one of the circular's most important recipients. Yet when the morning of July 1 came, Reynolds continued to push his infantry towards Gettysburg—towards cavalry divisional commander John Buford, who had pleaded for help the

Meade headquartered in a home (below) in Taneytown as he drew up his plans for Pipe Creek. The unfolding situation in Gettysburg forced him to reassess his plans. Today, a sign marks the spot (left). (cchs, pg)

day before. The actions of Reynolds show the movements of a man who was thinking offensively—aggressively even—as contrasted with the defensive nature of Meade's circular.

By the early afternoon of July 1, Meade had received word of Reynold's death and the growing-nature of the fight at Gettysburg. At that point, Meade knew it was unlikely the Pipe Creek line would be established, and he pressed men and materials towards the battle. The plan was abandoned without ever being tested.

Taneytown Memorial Park hosts several markers explaining the movements of Meade's army. (pg)

Some historians have criticized Meade's Pipe Creek Circular, proclaiming that it showcases a trepid, hesitant commander who feared a meeting with Robert E. Lee. This is simply not true. When the circular was written, Meade had only been in command of the army—the largest army in the United States—for three days, and he was trying to find a way to rein his forces in on one location. Meade must surely be given credit for quickly adapting to the scene at Gettysburg by ordering more troops to the town, and upon arriving there early on the morning of July 2, committing to the fight.

Other commanders of the Army of the Potomac had months to plan and become acclimated with their forces, yet even then, they were defeated one by one. Meade, on the other hand, took command of the Army of the Potomac on June 28, thought of the Pipe Creek Circular on June 30, abandoned that plan on July 1, and fought and won the battle of Gettysburg. They were the six most-hectic days of George Gordon Meade's life, and he did much better than anyone could have expected of him.

RYAN QUINT, *born and raised in Maine, moved to Virginia to earn a degree in history from the University of Mary Washington in Fredericksburg.*

The Peace Light Memorial
APPENDIX H
BY DAN WELCH

Fifty years after the guns fell silent, after the Union dead had been buried in the Soldiers' National Cemetery, after Lincoln called for a "new birth of freedom," veterans of the Blue and Gray returned once more to Gettysburg. In the decades following the conclusion of the war, acres of ground had been bought and preserved at Gettysburg, and hundreds of monuments had been erected to regiments and officers who had fought during the three-day engagement. Great reunions had been held, and tent cities sprung up on once-contested ground periodically over the close of the 19th century. Thus, in 1913, the 50th anniversary of the battle, yet another reunion took place.

Out of the reunion came more than just speeches and new monuments dedicated on the former fields of glory. A great feeling of peace and reconciliation pervaded speeches and headlines of coverage from the event. Veterans of both armies sought to capture these feelings with a Peace Memorial that would commemorate "that wonderful meeting of 'friendship and good-will.'" By the end of July 1913, veterans with these sentiments had organized and had begun seeking support for the idea.

Not long after the last veterans of the great reunion had returned home and the small town of Gettysburg had returned to a feeling of normalcy, the Gettysburg Peace Memorial Association was formed. The organization announced that it had only one purpose: "to secure an appropriation from Congress for a suitable Peace Memorial."

Filling the ranks of the Gettysburg Peace Memorial Association were many notable veterans, such as Joshua Chamberlain, Evander Law, John Nicholson, Andrew Cowan, and Elisha Rhodes. With key organizational structures in place, the association lost no time in pushing forward with their agenda. By December 1913, H.R. 11112 was introduced to the second session of the 63rd Congress. In the resolution, it was enacted "That a Commission is hereby created . . . charged with the duty of determining and procuring a suitable location and erection thereon of an appropriate memorial on the battlefield of Gettysburg, to commemorate the reunion of the veterans of the Union and Confederate armies on the Fiftieth Anniversary of that battle. . . ."

Despite an energetic start, it was another 25 years before the realization of a Peace Monument on the Gettysburg battlefield.

The opposite side of the Eternal Light Peace Memorial declares it to be "[a]n enduring light to guide us in unity and fellowship." (cm)

As many as half a million people turned out for the dedication of the Eternal Light Peace Memorial, but the VIPs of the event were the 1,800 Civil War veterans—most of them in their nineties—who attended. (gnmp)

In 1935, the Pennsylvania legislature authorized a commission and appropriated funds to begin planning for the 75th anniversary of the battle in 1938. As the commission pushed forward with planning, a focal point of the several-days-long event would finally be the dedication of a Peace Monument. Referred to as the Eternal Light Peace Memorial, the original intent to commemorate the feelings of friendship of the 1913 reunion had expanded to one where "the memory of every man, woman and child, North and South, who participated in anyway in the War Between the States" was to be honored by this memorial.

Although a design still had not been decided upon, the idea of an eternal light or flame had been constant since its original conception. The Pennsylvania State Commission report noted, "The light will not be in the form of a beacon. On the contrary it will be a flaming glow, casting a bright flare skyward as a symbol of peace, unity, harmony and good-fellowship in these United States."

Three years later, on February 14, 1938, groundbreaking ceremonies signaled the start of construction on the project. The 40-foot-tall memorial was estimated to cost nearly $60,000 with monies raised from Pennsylvania, New York, Wisconsin, Indiana, Tennessee, Virginia, Illinois, and the federal government to help cover the cost of the construction and materials. Alabama Rockwood limestone and Maine granite comprised the main building materials for the memorial, a symbolic gesture. On June 15, 1938, the memorial was completed and awaited its official dedication, scheduled for July 3.

Crowds gathered early on the morning of July 3, 1938, to see the dedication and monument unveiling later that day. Estimates of the crowd size by the time the official program began ranged from as low as 150,000 to more than 500,000. Highways and roads for miles around leading to Gettysburg turned into gridlock, some visitors not arriving until after the dedication was over.

Sheltered stands had been constructed next to the monument to provide priority and comfortable seating for Civil War veterans and their personal attendants. When each busload of veterans arrived to take their place throughout the afternoon, "they were greeted by tumultuous cheers and applause," noted Alexander Kendrick, a reporter for the *Philadelphia Inquirer*.

At 4:30 p.m., pre-ceremony activities began with an hour-long concert performed by the United States Marine Corps band. When the concert concluded, artillery placed on nearby Oak Ridge opened fire with a 21-gun salute as the main speaker arrived at the monument escorted by a cavalry troop. The unveiling and dedication ceremony of the Eternal Light Peace Memorial had officially begun. The time was a little past 5:30 p.m.

The ceremony opened with a prayer given by the United Confederate Veterans chaplain J. J. Methvin. Following the brief religious message, state senator, chairman of the reunion planning commission, and Adams County native John Rice introduced Pennsylvania Governor George Earle. At the conclusion of his remarks, Earle introduced the main speaker—and reason for such high attendance at the unveiling, President Franklin Delano Roosevelt.

The president's speech was short, much like Lincoln's decades before. He intoned the themes of sectional reconciliation. "They [the veterans] are brought here by the memories of old divided loyalties, but they meet here in united loyalty to a united cause which the unfolding years have made it easier to see." Roosevelt continued

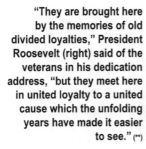

"They are brought here by the memories of old divided loyalties," President Roosevelt (right) said of the veterans in his dedication address, "but they meet here in united loyalty to a united cause which the unfolding years have made it easier to see." (**)

this motif when he said, "All of them we honor, not asking under which flag they fought then—thankful that they stand together under one flag now."

But Roosevelt also wove into his speech challenges that the country was facing internally as well as threats that potentially loomed on the horizon. He alluded to the rise of the American Nazi and Communist parties as an internal conflict to be dealt with using reason and not steel, and he sought "to save for our common country opportunity and security for citizens in a free society." He repeatedly suggested that we face our challenges head on without the use of violence, weaponry, and war—clearly foreshadowing fears of events to come in Europe. "Here in our land we give thanks that, avoiding war, we seek our ends through the peaceful processes of popular government under the Constitution," he said.

Despite strong appeals to the isolationist policies of the country in the tone and tenor of some of his words, Roosevelt cited Lincoln when he noted that if there was indeed a challenge to this country, its form of government, or its people, we would not back down. "[Lincoln] understood that battle there must be; that when a challenge to constituted government is thrown down, the people must in self-defense take it up; that the fight must be fought through to a decision so clear that it is accepted as beyond recall."

Following the conclusion of Roosevelt's speech, it was time for the monument to be unveiled from behind the massive American flag draped from its top. Two Civil War veterans had the honor of pulling the cord that dropped the flag. George N. Lockwood, a 92-year-old Union veteran, and A. G. Harris, a 91-year-old Confederate veteran, worked in harmony to not only

At the dedication of the Peace Light Memorial: the 48-star flag came down and the band played. (gnmp)

reveal the monument, but also to "touch the device that set the flames leaping in the urn atop the memorial."

The two veterans had revealed a monument designed by French-born Philadelphia architect and designer Paul Phillipe Cret. The designer, already well known for numerous other war memorials, including the National Memorial Arch at Valley Forge, was not the only one to work on the monument, however. Lee Lawrie, a German-born immigrant to the United States, had become one of the foremost architectural sculptors in the country in those years before World War II. Best known for his statue of *Atlas* in Rockefeller Center on 5th Avenue in New York City, Lawrie provided the bas-relief of the two women on the shaft of the monument. "Standing beside a young and hopeful America," one interpretation of the scene notes, "Columbia points out the broad horizons and high destiny which are God's constant challenges to noble endeavor." Other interpretations of the memorial's sculpted figures fulfill the reconciliation theme of the memorial, "the peace and good will existing between north and south." The traditional symbol of the United States, the eagle, completes the bas-relief.

Two inscriptions also adorn the shaft. One, about the theme and symbolism of the memorial itself: "An enduring light to guide us in unity and fellowship." The other, by Lincoln: "With firmness in the right as God gives us to see the right."

As the crowd was finally able to take in the revealed monument and the ceremony came to a conclusion, the last official reunion of the Blue and Gray at Gettysburg ended.

The history of the Eternal Peace Light Memorial does not end with the conclusion of its dedication ceremony, however. The most notable aspect of the memorial, its eternal flame, fills a large portion of its enduring story. Originally envisioned by both the Gettysburg Peace Memorial Association and the 1938 reunion planning commission to be eternal, the flame has faced numerous challenges to fulfill its symbolic mission.

Two days after its dedication, on July 5, 1938, *The Evening Sun*, a newspaper from nearby Hanover, Pennsylvania, reported that the eternal light "will not burn with a 'perpetual' flame." The story continued to state that contributions to fund an eternal flame supplied by natural gas had fallen fall short of that needed for the flame to burn both night and day. Thus, "the stream of natural gas will be shut off at 6 o'clock each morning and will be lighted at 6 o'clock each evening, during the summer," the paper reported, and, during winter months, "the flame will burn 16 hours in each 24."

During the energy crisis of the 1970s, the gas flame was replaced by an electric lamp. (gnmp)

Just 25 years later, the gas flame was extinguished altogether. As a gesture of energy conservation, the flame was extinguished as the country became crippled by the gas crisis of the 1970s. Relit briefly during the 1976 bicentennial of the United States, the flame remained extinguished until July 1, 1978, when a sodium vapor lamp was placed within the urn and powered by electricity.

Finally, on July 3, 1988, 50 years after its dedication, the original intent of the eternal flame became reality once again when the flame was rekindled.

The memorial was also the setting for another presidential visit, inspiring a historical legacy with a connection to Arlington National Cemetery. On March 31, 1963, President John F. Kennedy, along with several family and friends, left from Camp David,

DAN WELCH *worked for the National Park Service at Gettysburg National Military Park for six seasons as a seasonal park ranger in the Interpretation Division. He currently serves as the education programs coordinator for the Gettysburg Foundation.*

Maryland, and headed northward to tour the Gettysburg battlefield. The Kennedy entourage visited many of the more popular spots on the battlefield, the High Water Mark, Little Round Top, the Wheatfield, and the North Carolina monument before ending their tour at the Eternal Peace Light Memorial. It was here that one of the most iconic photos of the presidential visit was taken.

The memorial, as seen by the president and the first lady, reportedly served as inspiration for Mrs. Kennedy in the design of her husband's final resting place in Arlington National Cemetery following his assassination in Texas.

Today, the Eternal Peace Light Memorial serves as a silent witness to history. Each year, nearly 1.6 million visitors stand at its base and gaze at the eternal flame. It was created as a symbol of the feelings of reconciliation and reunion—a theme ever present in the memory of the war since the Gilded Age and one that continues to shape our retelling of the war even today.

One of the most iconic images of President John F. Kennedy captures him and his party gazing up at the Peace Light during a March 1963 visit to the battlefield. (gd)

Order of Battle

THE FIRST DAY AT GETTYSBURG

The order of battle reflects only those units engaged on July 1, 1863.

ARMY OF THE POTOMAC
Maj. Gen. George G. Meade

LEFT WING

FIRST ARMY CORPS: Maj. Gen. John Reynolds (k),
Maj. Gen. Abner Doubleday
FIRST DIVISION: Brig. Gen. James Wadsworth
First Brigade (Iron Brigade): Brig. Gen. Solomon Meredith (w),
Col. William Robinson
19th Indiana · 24th Michigan · 2nd Wisconsin · 6th Wisconsin · 7th Wisconsin

Second Brigade: Brig. Gen. Lysander Cutler
7th Indiana · 76th New York · 84th New York (14th Militia) · 95th New York · 147th New York · 56th Pennsylvania

SECOND DIVISION: Brig. Gen. John C. Robinson
First Brigade: Brig. Gen. Gabriel Paul
16th Maine · 18th Massachusetts · 94th New York · 104th New York · 107th Pennsylvania

Second Brigade: Brig. Gen. Henry Baxter
12th Massachusetts · 83rd New York (9th Militia) · 97th New York · 11th Pennsylvania · 88th Pennsylvania · 90th Pennsylvania

THIRD DIVISION: Maj. Gen. Abner Doubleday, Brig. Gen. Thomas Rowley
First Brigade Col. Chapman Biddle (w), Brig. Gen. Thomas Rowley
80th New York (20th Militia) · 121st Pennsylvania · 142nd Pennsylvania · 151st Pennsylvania

Second Brigade: Col. Roy Stone (w), Col. Langhorne Wister (w),
Col. Edmund Dana
143rd Pennsylvania · 149th Pennsylvania · 150th Pennsylvania

Third Brigade is not engaged on July 1.

Artillery Brigade: Col. Charles S. Wainwright
Battery B, 2nd Maine Light · Battery E, 5th Maine Light · Battery L, 1st New York Light
Battery B, 1st Pennsylvania Light · Battery B, 4th United States

ELEVENTH ARMY CORPS: Maj. Gen. Oliver Otis Howard
FIRST DIVISION: Brig. Gen. Francis Barlow (w), Brig. Gen. Adelbert Ames
First Brigade: Col. Leopold Von Gilsa
41st New York · 54th New York · 68th New York · 153rd Pennsylvania

Second Brigade: Brig. Gen. Adelbert Ames, Col. Andrew Harris
17th Connecticut · 25th Ohio · 75th Ohio · 107th Ohio

SECOND DIVISION: Brig. Gen. Adolph von Steinwehr
First Brigade: Col. Charles Coster
134th New York · 154th New York · 27th Pennsylvania · 73rd Pennsylvania

Second Brigade: Col. Orland Smith
33rd Massachusetts · 136th New York · 55th Ohio · 73rd Ohio

THIRD DIVISION: Maj. Gen. Carl Schurz
First Brigade: Brig. Gen. Alexander Schimmelfenning (m), Col. George von Amsburg
82nd Illinois · 45th New York · 157th New York · 61st Ohio · 74th Pennsylvania

Second Brigade: Col. Wladimir Krzyzanowski
58th New York · 119th New York · 82nd Ohio · 75th Pennsylvania · 26th Wisconsin

Artillery Brigade: Maj. Thomas Osborn
Battery I, 1st New York Light · 13th Battery, New York Light · Battery I, 1st Ohio Light
Battery K, 1st Ohio Light · Battery G, 4th United States

CAVALRY CORPS: Maj. Gen. Alfred Pleasonton
FIRST DIVISION: Brig. John Buford
First Brigade: Col. William Gamble
8th Illinois · 12th Illinois (four companies) · 3rd Indiana (six companies) · 8th New York

Second Brigade: Col. Thomas C. Devin
6th New York · 9th New York · 17th Pennsylvania · 3rd West Virginia (two companies)

Third Brigade is not engaged on July 1.

Artillery: Battery A, 2nd United States

*   *   *

ARMY OF NORTHERN VIRGINIA
Gen. Robert E. Lee

SECOND CORPS: Lt. Gen. Richard S. Ewell
EARLY'S DIVISION: Maj. Gen. Jubal Early
Hays's Brigade: Brig. Gen. Harry T. Hays
5th Louisiana · 6th Louisiana · 7th Louisiana · 8th Louisiana · 9th Louisiana

Smith's Brigade: Brig. Gen. William Smith
31st Virginia · 49th Virginia · 52nd Virginia

Hoke's Brigade: Col. Isaac Avery
6th North Carolina · 21st North Carolina · 57th North Carolina

Gordon's Brigade: Brig. Gen. John B. Gordon
13th Georgia · 26th Georgia · 31st Georgia · 38th Georgia · 60th Georgia · 61st Georgia

Artillery: Lt. Col. Hillary Jones
*Charlottesville (Virginia) Artillery · Courtney (Virginia) Artillery · Louisiana Guard Artillery
Staunton (Virginia) Artillery*

RODES' DIVISION: Maj. Gen. Robert E. Rodes
Daniel's Brigade: Brig. Gen. Junius Daniel
*32nd North Carolina · 43rd North Carolina · 45th North Carolina · 53rd North Carolina
2nd North Carolina Battalion*

Iverson's Brigade: Brig. Gen. Alfred Iverson
5th North Carolina · 12th North Carolina · 20th North Carolina · 23rd North Carolina

Doles' Brigade: Brig. Gen. George Doles
4th Georgia · 12th Georgia · 21st Georgia · 44th Georgia

Iverson's Brigade: Brig. Gen. Stephen Ramseur
2nd North Carolina · 4th North Carolina · 14th North Carolina · 30th North Carolina

O'Neal's Brigade: Col. Edward O'Neal
3rd Alabama · 5th Alabama · 6th Alabama · 12th Alabama · 26th Alabama

Artillery: Lt. Col. Thomas Carter
*Jeff Davis (Alabama) Artillery · King William (Virginia) Artillery · Morris (Virginia) Artillery
Orange (Virginia) Artillery*

THIRD CORPS: Lt. Gen. Ambrose P. Hill
HETH'S DIVISION: Maj. Gen. Henry Heth (w), Brig. Gen. James J. Pettigrew
First Brigade: Brig. Gen. James J. Pettigrew, Col. J.K. Marshall
11th North Carolina · 26th North Carolina · 47th North Carolina · 52nd North Carolina

Second Brigade: Col. John Brockenbrough
40th Virginia · 47th Virginia · 55th Virginia · 22nd Virginia Battalion

Third Brigade: Brig. Gen. James Archer (c), Col. Birkett Fry
13th Alabama · 5th Alabama Battalion · 1st Tennessee (Provisional Army) · 7th Tennessee
14th Tennessee

Fourth Brigade: Brig. Gen. Joseph R. Davis
2nd Mississippi · 11th Mississippi · 42nd Mississippi · 55th North Carolina

Artillery: Lt. Col. John J. Garnett
Donaldsonville (Louisiana) Artillery · Huger (Virginia) Artillery · Lewis (Virginia) Artillery
Norfolk Light Artillery Blues

PENDER'S DIVISION: Maj. Gen. William D. Pender
First Brigade: Col. Abner Perrin
1st South Carolina (Provisional Army) · 1st South Carolina Rifles · 12th South Carolina
13th South Carolina 14th South Carolina

Second Brigade: Brig. Gen. James Lane
7th North Carolina · 18th North Carolina · 28th North Carolina · 33rd North Carolina
37th North Carolina

Third Brigade: Brig. Gen. Edward L. Thomas
14th Georgia · 35th Georgia · 45th Georgia · 49th Georgia

Fourth Brigade: Brig. Gen. Alfred Scales
13th North Carolina · 16th North Carolina · 22nd North Carolina · 34th North Carolina
38th North Carolina

Artillery: Maj. William T. Poague
Albemarle (Virginia) Artillery · Charlotte (North Carolina) Artillery
Madison (Mississippi) Artillery · Virginia (Brooke's) Battery

ARTILLERY RESERVE: Col. R. Lindsay Walker
McIntosh's Battalion: Maj. D. G. McIntosh
Danville (Virginia) Artillery · Hardaway (Alabama) Artillery · 2nd Rockbridge (Virginia)
Artillery · Virginia (Johnson's) Battery

Pegram's Battalion: Maj. William Pegram
Crenshaw (Virginia) Artillery · Fredericksburg (Virginia) Artillery · Letcher (Virginia) Artillery
Pee Dee (South Carolina) Artillery · Purcell (Virginia) Artillery

Suggested Reading
THE FIRST DAY AT GETTYSBURG

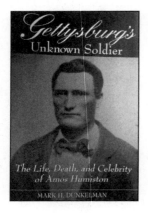

Gettysburg's Unknown Soldier: The Life, Death, and Celebrity of Amos Humiston
Mark H. Dunkelman
Praeger, 1999
ISBN-13: 978-0275962944

Unknown at the time of his death, Amos Humiston became a national celebrity months after his unidentified body was found on the battlefield. His story remains one of Gettysburg's most popular—and sublime. Dunkelman, who had an ancestor that served with Humiston, has devoted his considerable career to documenting the regiment's history.

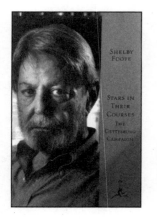

The Stars in Their Courses: The Gettysburg Campaign
Shelby Foote
Modern Library, 1994
ISBN-13: 978-0679601128

The Stars in Their Courses excerpts the Gettysburg section from Foote's three-volume *The Civil War: A Narrative.* While historians criticized Foote's lack of footnotes, *Stars* emphasizes story and craftsmanship, making it the most beautifully written book about Gettysburg—and an artful entre for those who want human experience over microtactical detail.

First Day at Gettysburg: Crisis at the Crossroads
Warren W. Hassler, Jr.
University Alabama Press, 2010
ISBN-13: 978-0817356170

The First Day at Gettysburg
Crisis at the Crossroads
WARREN W. HASSLER JR.

Hassler gets right to it with a crisply written account of the first day's battle. He sets up the battle quickly and offers only bare biographical information, but his use of first-person accounts and other primary sources gives his narrative excellent color. Not as in-depth as other accounts, Hassler trades detail for readability.

Those Damned Black Hats: The Iron Brigade in the Gettysburg Campaign
Lance Herdegen
Savas Beatie, 2010
ISBN: 978-1932714838

Those Damned Black Hats!
THE IRON BRIGADE IN THE GETTYSBURG CAMPAIGN
LANCE J. HERDEGEN

The Iron Brigade is one of the best-known units of the Army of the Potomac. At Gettysburg on July 1, they were some of the first Federal infantry regiments to reach the battlefield. Later in the afternoon, these Westerners were heavily engaged with James Pettigrew's North Carolinians in Herbst Woods. In Those Damned Black Hats, Herdegen, a recognized expert on the Iron Brigade, recounts the unit's early days in Virginia and chronicles their pivotal actions during the Gettysburg Campaign.

The First Day at Gettysburg: Essays on Confederate and Union Leadership
Gary Gallagher, ed.
Kent State University Press, 1993
ISBN-13: 978-0873384575

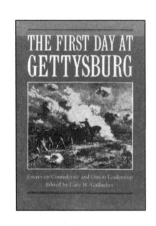

THE FIRST DAY AT GETTYSBURG
Essays on Confederate and Union Leadership
Edited by Gary W. Gallagher

Gallagher, the hardest-working Civil War historian in academia, has dedicated much of his career to bridging the gap between the academy and the public. In this collection of essays, he brings together an all-star line-up of historians—Alan Nolan, Robert Krick, A. Wilson Greene, and Gallagher himself—to evaluate some of the key command decisions from the first day of battle.

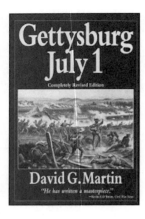

Gettysburg July 1
David G. Martin
Da Capo Press (reprint edition), 2003
ISBN-13: 978-0306812408

Martin's exhaustive book casts a wide net, rewinding to Lee's departure from Fredericksburg on June 3 and then getting into the weeds once he gets into Pennsylvania. His attention to individual actions makes the book more episodic than most narratives of the battle. The original version of the book is legendary for some factual gaffs, but the revised edition has cleaned them up.

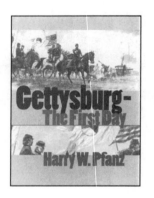

Gettysburg: The First Day
Harry W. Pfanz
University of North Carolina Press, 2001
ISBN-13: 978-0807871317 (hardcover)

Pfanz, the former chief historian for Gettysburg National Military Park, is as intimately familiar with the battlefield as he is with the primary sources. His study of the first day is deeply researched and intricately detailed, making it a must-have for anyone who wants an in-depth microtactical account of the events of July 1, 1863.

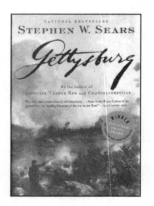

Gettysburg
Stephen Sears
Mariner Books, 2004
ISBN-13: 978-0618485383 (paperback)

This bestseller won the 2003 Fletcher Pratt Award for best book on the Civil War, but its selection as a *New York Times* Notable Book and the *Los Angeles Times* Best Book of the Year speak to its accessibility to a wide audience. Like his other battle studies, Sears weaves plenty of primary sources with highly readable prose to create a page-turning narrative. This is the best single-volume overview of the battle available.

The Story of Robert E. Lee's Headquarters
Timothy H. Smith
Thomas Publications, 1996
ISBN-13: 978-0939631858

Don't let the third-rate publishing job fool you: it doesn't do justice to Timoth Smith's excellent history of Mary Thompson's house. Smith, a Licensed Battlefield Guide, takes readers behind the scenes with a meticulously researched biography of the building and the people who've occupied it.

"The Devil's to Pay": John Buford at Gettysburg
Eric Wittenberg
Savas Beatie, 2014
ISBN-13: 978-1611212082

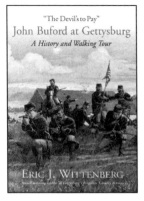

In a battle that had many heroes, few stand as tall as John Buford on the first day. Eric Wittenberg is *the* expert on Union cavalry, and *Devil* represents in many ways the culmination of his life's work. Carefully researched and lovingly drawn, Wittenberg's study of Buford stands as the definitive account of the cavalryman's legendary stand.

Plenty of Blame to Go Around: Jeb Stuart's Controversial Ride to Gettysburg
Eric J. Wittenberg and J. David Petruzzi
Savas Beatie, 2006
ISBN-13: 978-1932714838

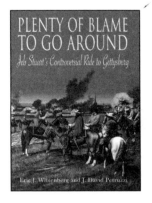

Among the most highly debated aspects of the Gettysburg campaign were the exploits of J.E.B. Stuart and his Confederate cavalry. Absent from Lee's army for much of the campaign, Stuart led his "Invincibles" on a ride through eastern Virginia and into Maryland before joining Robert E. Lee at Gettysburg on the second day of the battle. In this richly detailed account, Wittenberg and Petruzzi, authorities on Civil War cavalry operations, recount Stuart's ride, including the engagements at Hanover and Hunterstown, and thoroughly examine the arguments and controversies surrounding the event.

About the Authors

Chris Mackowski, Ph.D., is editor-in-chief of Emerging Civil War. He splits his time between western New York, where he teaches writing at St. Bonaventure University, and Fredericksburg, Virginia, where he's the historian-in-residence at Stevenson Ridge, a historic property on the Spotsylvania battlefield. He has also worked at Fredericksburg and Spotsylvania National Military Park (FSNMP).

Kristopher D. White is chief historian for Emerging Civil War, a historian for the Penn-Trafford Recreation Board, and a continuing education instructor for the Community College of Allegheny County near Pittsburgh. White is a graduate of Norwich University with a M.A. in Military History, as well as a graduate of California University of Pennsylvania with a B.A. in History. For five years, he served as a staff military historian at FSNMP, where he still volunteers his services. For a short time he was a member of the Association of Licensed Battlefield Guides at Gettysburg.

Chris and Kris are co-founders of Emerging Civil War. They have also authored or co-authored more than a dozen books on the Civil War—nine of them for the Emerging Civil War Series. Their writing has also appeared in *Civil War Times, America's Civil War, Blue & Gray,* and *Hallowed Ground.* They are also editors of Engaging the Civil War, a book series published in conjunction with Southern Illinois University Press.

Daniel Davis is managing editor of Emerging Civil War. He is a graduate of Longwood University with a B.A. in Public History. Dan has worked as a historian at both Appomattox Court House National Historic Site and at FSNMP. He resides in Fredericksburg, Virginia, with his wife Katy and Beagle mix, Bayla. With Phillip Greenwalt, he is the co-author of *Bloody Autumn: The Shenandoah Valley Campaign of 1864, Hurricane from the Heavens: The Battle of Cold Harbor, May 26-June 5, 1864,* and *Calamity in Carolina: The Battles of Averasboro and Bentonville.*

Read their blog at www.emergingcivilwar.com.